Volume 1, No. 1 * Fall 2010 *
ISSN 2158-9623

Journal of

Black

Masculinity

The Journal of Black Masculinity

Copyright © 2010 GES Publishing Group/GES LLC.

ISBN 978-1-60910-647-8

ISSN 2158-9623

Printed in the United States of America.

Volume 1, No. 1
Fall 2010

Journal of Black Masculinity

C. P. Gause, Founder and Editor

The Journal of Black Masculinity is a peer-reviewed international publication providing multiple discoursed and multiple-discipline-based analyses of issues and/or perspectives with regard to black masculinities. The journal will accept empirical, theoretical, and literary scholarship as well as essays, poetry, and creative art. Submissions from multiple disciplines beyond the humanities and social sciences are encouraged. *The Journal of Black Masculinity* is published three times a year and has a ten percent (10%) acceptance rate. *The Journal of Black Masculinity* also publishes special issues on a periodic basis with guest editors focusing on themed issues.

Manuscript submissions, books for review, and correspondence concerning all editorial matters should be sent to: C. P. Gause, Editor, *The Journal of Black Masculinity,* using the contact information below. Manuscripts submitted for publication will be peer-reviewed.
Manuscripts should be submitted in electronic form and should not exceed 25 pages in length (including endnotes and references). Authors should follow the *APA Publication Manual*, 6th edition (APA Press, 2010). A style guide for preparing manuscripts can be viewed and/or copied from the *JBM* website at http://www.blackmasculinity.com

GES LLC
2309 W. Cone Blvd. Suite 142
Greensboro, NC 27408
www.blackmasculinity.com
www.drcpgause.com
drcpgause@gmail.com
336.509.6171

Journal of Black Masculinity

Editor & Founder: C. P. Gause, University of North
                               Carolina-Greensboro

Book Editor: Robert Randolph, University of North
                               Carolina-Greensboro

Copy & Layout Editor: Jean K. Rosales, University of North
                               Carolina-Greensboro

Associate Editor in Residence: Ruth Reese, University of North
                               Carolina-Greensboro

Associate Editor in Residence: Pamela Fitzpatrick, University of North
                               Carolina-Greensboro

v

The Journal of Black Masculinity, Vol. 1, No. 1, Fall 2010

Toby Jenkins
George Mason University

Michael Jennings
University of Texas at San Antonio

Ralph Soney
Roanoke-Chowan Community College

Lemuel Watson
Northern Illinois University

Journal of Black Masculinity

Volume 1, No. 1   Fall 2010

Contents

From the Beginnings-Ripping the Veil by Queering Black Masculinities

C. P. Gause, Ph.D.

Welcome to the inaugural issue of *The Journal of Black Masculinity.*

Presently, in today's global community, we find ourselves bombarded on a 24-hour daily basis with mediated imagery and sounds that shape our values, belief systems, and moral structures. The constant bombardment of popular culture on our daily existence informs our global identities, as well as national identities. Throughout our global history, education has been viewed as the un-kept promise of many societies and democracies.

Scholars, researchers, and policymakers continue to inform our communities that children of color and children in poverty are being left behind, particularly the "black male." Many scholars and policymakers continue to limit the analyses of black masculinity to detached statistical data and reports devoid of the authentic (re)presentations of the voice and performance of global masculinities across multiple landscapes. There exists a full range of gender expressions witnessed by all, globally; however, given the power of the media, the only representation often presented of black males is the duffle bag boy—drug runner and money carries; the thug—an aggressive, no-holds-barred bad boy; and the convict—a prison lifer, always in and out of jail. The underlying messages in these images are ones of heteronormativity, homophobia, and patriarchy.

The constructions of aggressive male identities are still prevalent because tolerance and not affirmation of the "other" continues to be the accepted norm in our society, and schools are microcosmic representations of our larger society. The affirmation of queering masculinities by society as a whole would expand white male-dominated constructions of masculinity beyond the heteronormative. Queering masculine characteristics would move beyond typically viewed/accepted "male" behaviors and embrace behaviors of all members of the global community regardless of sexually identified, gender-perceived, and biologically confirmed positionalities.

The political disturbances and cultural representations of black masculinity in popular culture require new and different readings and contextualizations. Currently, black masculinity is rooted in masculine hero worship in the case of rappers and as naturalized and commodified in the case of athletes. The combination of these two has yielded a new Public Enemy Number One, a sadistic and masochistic heterosexist black masculine cyborg, devoid of emotion, thought, and remorse.

The current construction/representation of the black male brings together the dominant institutions of (white) masculine power and identity—criminal justice system, the police, and the news media—to protect (white) Americans from harm. The heavily policed and illuminated image of the black male is the object of adolescent intrigue, fascination, and commodification. By drawing on deeply felt moral pains presently regarding crime, violence, gangs, and drugs, numerous black entertainers—namely athletes and rap artists—have rewritten the historic tropes of black masculinity from provider and protector to pusher and pimp.

This corrosive nihilistic construction of maleness reifies notions of (hyper)sexuality, insensitivity, and criminality, which serve as the new tropes of fascination and fear for the dominant culture. It becomes a veil of black masculinity, a veil in which, at times during my life, I was complicit. This is why I interrogate my own identity by queering black masculinity.

We say, "Not so!" We believe black males across the global Diaspora are one of the most powerful creations ever known to our humanity. As a testament to this belief, we have brought together scholars, dancers, teachers, poets, educators, Hip Hop artists, policymakers, spoken-word performers, politicians, and researchers to celebrate and affirm our black masculinities in this issue. The texts produced by these individuals, in this issue, serve as the counter-narratives to mediated hegemonic constructions of the bestial, hypersexualized, aggressive, co-opted, and commodified cyborg that is the black male. The authors represent multilingual, multi-ethnic, and nonconforming Eurocentric gender identities and are considered national and international scholars and scholars-of-promise.

I would like to thank the editorial review board, the editorial advisory committee, the faculty, staff, students, and administration of the University of North Carolina at Greensboro and the University Libraries for their contributions and support. I hope you find this issue and subsequent issues intellectually thought provoking and stimulating.

C. P. Gause, Ph.D.

www.drcpgause.com
www.blackmasculinity.com
drcpgause@gmail.com

Still

Aubrey Lynch, II

Woodhaven, Michigan and
the Alvin Ailey American Dance Theater

I am still
Loving still
Moving Still
Being still

You are still
Your body still
My soul still
My thoughts still

Still in me
The will in me
The dreams I see
Will always be

We cannot be
Could never be
What lives in me
Your gifts to me

Through me
Though I am still
In your love to me
I am dancing still

For Barry Martin who choreographed from a wheelchair and was friend and mentor to Aubrey Lynch II.

Biography

Aubrey Lynch II from Woodhaven, Michigan danced with Alvin Ailey American Dance Theater and then went on to appear in TV commercials, print ads, movies, and music videos. Mr. Lynch was an original cast member of the Tony Award-winning Broadway musical, Disney's *The Lion King,* and acted as the production's dance captain, associate choreographer, and then associate producer overseeing all creative aspects of all *Lion King* productions worldwide. Currently on faculty at The Ailey School and a certified life coach, Aubrey has developed his own life transformative workshop program, *The Aubrey Lynch Show. Experience.*

Brother

TLH

Day in Day out, I see my Brother
Standing on the Corner
Day in Day out, I see him running from the Black and Blue
As I drive pass, I wonder why he choose to live a life of crime
That gives no other reward
But jail time

Is it because he had no choice,
No other way? I wonder why
Because we both came from the same place
And when I say the same place
I mean the same ghetto
The same home life
We both came from the same family

One Mother…more children
Yet people think we come from
Two different worlds

My brother, you think he comes from a world of darkness
Where there is no sense of right or wrong
Just only the sense of survival
And I a world of light where there is a sense of right and wrong

How can brothers, brought up in the same home
Given the same morals of life be so far apart
Is society to blame or is it the lack of trying on ones part

Did he not have the same chances as I?
Or did I have more options then he
And if so, then it is society who should be blamed

For it was society who brought the youth
To the world of light or maybe there aren't two worlds
But one world where half is light and the other is dark and if so
Where do we start to bring this world to light?

Biography

TLH was born in Ohio. He enjoys writing in his spare time. He is a great cook and excellent barber.

"BF" (Black Face)
C. P. Gause, Ph.D.

Mahogany skin
Face as black as coal
Your last thoughts
      To be free
My goal

The bond we shared
Our mothers bound
On my crying knees
You
Placed into the ground

Love unimaginable
Our secrets
Beheld
Your spirit spoke to me
Even from jail

I knew
You knew
      And you loved many
It wasn't about the money
You said
Not even one penny

Confessions I heard
You shared them in confidence

And confessed the Lord your savior
I even sought repentance

Miss you still
Yet see you everyday
So many black men
Dying
And losing their way

Your life
A message
To the bold
Even the few
The day the bullet hit
Cold no more
Yet we knew

Hip Hop Culture: A Way to Be Black

Eloise Tan, Ph.D.

Dublin City University
Dublin, Ireland

Abstract

It is necessary to understand what young black men mean when they say, "I am Hip Hop," so that we can understand how Hip Hop culture affects how they negotiate their identities as young adults. Throughout this paper, we see evidence of the familiar contradictions within Hip Hop culture dealing with issues of gender, race, and education (Alim, 2004; Hill, 2008; Rose, 2008), but we also see how two participants—Jeffrey and Everson—intricately re-work their identity construction in Hip Hop in different ways from when they first came to Hip Hop. My research is based upon ethnographic work with the core team of 13 youth, as well as other Hip Hop youth artists. Taken together, the portraits of Jeffrey and Everson uncover what constructing identities in Hip Hop entails for some young black males and what a Hip Hop ideology might look like for them.

Hip Hop culture shares at least two important characteristics. First is the urban youth aesthetic, which is perhaps the most easily recognizable aspect of Hip Hop culture because it is expressed through music, clothing, language, and art. More than simply rap music and graffiti art, the urban youth aesthetic refers to visual and artistic expression of Hip Hop culture...

Second is urban youth experience, which is often shaped by economic isolation, poverty, and a struggle to 'make it out' of the trappings of urban ghettos (Ginwright, 2004, p. 31-32).

Hip Hop culture can be described as an emerging worldview among adults and youth born after 1965. This worldview is comprised of sharing beliefs, practices, and language all tied together by a common appreciation for the urban aesthetic. The above definition of Hip Hop culture is representative of how Hip Hop is conceptualized in academic circles. Ginwright's definition is neither definitive nor exhaustive, but rather it is a jumping off point from which to delve into how youth define Hip Hop through their commitments, style, and art. It is necessary to understand what young black men mean when they say, "I am Hip Hop," so that we can understand how Hip Hop culture affects how they negotiate their identities as young adults. Throughout this paper, we see evidence of the familiar contradictions within Hip Hop culture dealing with issues of race, masculinity and, identity (Alim, 2004; Hill, 2008; Low, Tan & Celemencki, forthcoming; Rose, 2008; Tan, 2009), but we also see how Jeffrey and Everson, two black male participants in a community Hip Hop documentary project, intricately re-work their identity construction in blackness and in Hip Hop in different ways from when they first came to Hip Hop. Thus, there is a sense of evolution within identity constructions in relation to Hip Hop evident in the snapshots of Jeffrey and Everson that have yet to be explored in the available literature of ethnographies of Hip Hop pedagogy.

Taken together, the portraits of Jeffrey and Everson uncover what constructing identities in Hip Hop entails for some young black males and what a Hip Hop ideology might look like for them.

Chronicle Creations Hip Hop Documentary

Beginning in late 2007, Chronicle Creations set out to create a participatory documentary with a team of Hip Hop youth artists in all four elements—b-boying, graffiti, MC-ing, and DJ-ing (Chang, 2005). Funded by the National Film Board of Canada[1] in 2008, Chronicle Creations began the participatory filmmaking process of creating a documentary about the role of Hip Hop culture in the lives of 13 youth and in the lives of Montreal youth more broadly. I worked with the two producers, two youth coordinators, and 13 participants as a participant-observer in their participatory filmmaking framework over four months in their pre-production working sessions.

My qualitative research is based upon that time working with the core team of 13 youth, as well as other Hip Hop youth artists whose commitment to the documentary ended at various points. I participated in weekly three-hour sessions where we discussed and planned the documentary, and I also conducted one-on-one interviews with participants following the four-month period of pre-production. I also accompanied the producers and the participants to various shooting locations such as for b-boy battles, graffiti sessions, or interviews. Within the core group of participants, the age range was 18-23 years old, with two females and eleven males. Nine of the participants self-identified as black, coming from different immigration routes. As each participant was an active artist in at least one of the four elements of Hip Hop, Hip Hop culture unified the 13 main participants who came from a variety of ethnic, linguistic and, transnational backgrounds. This paper focuses on two participants—Jeffrey and Everson—and how they performed and negotiated blackness in relation to their affiliations with Hip Hop culture. I provide two examples of moments where Jeffrey and Everson confront their performance of blackness in Hip Hop culture. These examples are taken from an interview with Jeffrey[2] and from a transcript of a discussion centering around Everson in the pre-production sessions where all 13 participants were present.

I initially intended the interviews to be a forum for individually de-briefing on participants' reflections on the learning process, but they emerged as a space where they could tell their story unencumbered by twelve other voices. Whereas the pre-production sessions provided each of them with a forum to discuss their views on Hip Hop culture today and where it will/should go tomorrow, the interviews gave them my undivided attention to listen to their past stories of Hip Hop and thus provided context for, and also sometimes contradicted, statements they made in pre-production.

Hip Hop Studies Up Here: "Translated Blackness"

The 13 participants represent a look at blackness and Hip Hop culture from a Canadian perspective. While there have been Canadian studies with Hip Hop youth and artists, they either focus explicitly on sociolinguistic practices (Forman, 2001; Ibrahim, 1999, 2004; Sarkar & Allen, 2007; Sarkar & Winer, 2006) or the participants' identity construction in relation to Hip Hop is not central to the study (Yon, 2000). Ethnographic studies conducted in Canada are needed to illustrate the complex ways in which Canadian youth negotiate and manipulate American pop cultural forms such as Hip Hop. Holland's (2001) argues that Canadian youth have not been treated as complex actors in cultural production, but rather as imitators of their Southern neighbors:

> Canadian youth have been viewed by Brake (1985) as: 1) being simply passive in their acceptance of American 'mass culture' and 2) possessing no popular cultural traditions themselves...It is more likely that Canadian youth (already a differentiated group as we have seen), have both selectively appropriated and refused elements of American popular culture. And that their identities and cultures are the products of a mixture of class, ethnic, gender and regional factors, and how they create not only their own indigenous culture, but how this is combined with the active consumption of global products. (p. 117)

Besides presenting more complex representations of Canadian youth and young adults, Canadian literature in critical Hip Hop pedagogy is timely especially to the Toronto context of schooling, given the recent debates for black-focused schooling in Toronto and the subsequent Toronto District School Board's approval for a school to be opened in September 2009. There is a definite sense of urgency behind the debate with findings from a 1995 Royal Commission that 40 percent of Grade 9 black students in the Greater Toronto Area were dropping out, coupled with statistics from the Toronto District School Board that 40 percent of Caribbean-born students drop out, and 32 percent from East Africa (Brown & Popplewell, 2008). Sackeyfio (2006) acknowledges the role that Hip Hop pedagogy could plan in Toronto's black-focused school: "In contrast with Hip Hop's placement on the periphery of schooling processes in mainstream schools, black-focused schools are in a better position to incorporate Hip Hop and its associated racial and cultural identities in the learning process" (p. 153).

Ibrahim's (1999, 2004) and Forman's (2005) work with immigrant and refugee students in Canada build on Alim's work by highlighting the complexity of identification for immigrant students. This Canadian focus situates a black Canadian immigrant identity against the hegemonic presence of black as it is reproduced in mainstream American media and Hip Hop media specifically. This Canadian immigrant experience of blackness can be seen as a "translated blackness" (Kelly, 2007). A discussion of blackness in North America has implications for non-black students as well. Yon's (2000) ethnographic work in an inner city Toronto high school displays the fluidity and contradictions of identity construction, many times in relation to constructions of blackness. One of Yon's participants who grew up in Jamaica and then was moved to Toronto in his teens shares his thoughts on some of his black peers who are African immigrants:

> I don't really consider them Black either. Seriously. I see a lot of them can speak Italian. They can speak a lot of languages. They're, like, dark on the outside but I guess we're all distinguishable.... For me, I see Black as being Jamaican... I guess it depends where they're from that I will consider them Black. (p. 87)

Here we see the importance of language in not only how one constructs identity but also how identity is perceived by others. Similar to Trevor's struggle with the boundaries of blackness, Yon shows how a participant Nina is frustrated as she is constantly being "read as black" although she sees herself as Spanish from Dominica (p. 70). Many of the participants in Chronicle Creations are well situated within Yon's contribution to the complexity of identity construction for diasporic students. Participants who immigrated to Montreal in their teens were familiar with Hip Hop from American imports into their home country and saw it as a vehicle through which to assert their kinship with an urban Canadian community. Forman (2005) makes a case that Somali youth arriving in Canada are predisposed to what being black means in North America as a result of their exposure:

> Somali youths quickly recognize that Hip Hop establishes many of the norms and values currently defining 'authentic' black identity among youths, and, moreover, they rapidly determine that these informal (that is, non-institutionally grounded) articulations of blackness are organized alternatively and often in radical opposition to the formally structured discourses of race and nation as they are communicated in the schools. (p. 16)

Whether or not this multicultural and transnational environment is specifically emblematic of the Canadian Hip Hop community is interesting especially considering some recent debates on the "multicultural-ness" of Hip Hop occurring in the States (Rose, 2008). While Yon's work is not commonly included in Hip Hop based education literature, the richness of his data on youth identity construction in relation to race, language, and gender benefits any study concerned with issues of blackness, identity, and Hip Hop.

Now we look at two poignant moments where Jeffrey and Everson discuss their male blackness in relation to their identities in Hip Hop culture. Jeffrey is an emcee who grew up in a suburb outside of Montreal, but has since moved to Montreal. Everson was one of the few participants who were not as serious about involvement in an element *per se*. Everson immigrated to Montreal from Brooklyn and has his roots in Haiti. Through Jeffrey's interview, we see how he consciously involved himself with Hip Hop as a way to mark him-self as "more black." Complementary to that, we see in a discussion with all participants how Everson challenges the group of participants to confront what weight blackness carries in Hip Hop culture and Hip Hop authenticity. Following these two "moments" of examination, I discuss what Jeffrey's and Everson's words mean for the identity project of black males in Hip Hop culture.

Pathways into Hip Hop

From stepping back and trying to understand how each participant entered their relationship with Hip Hop culture, it becomes clear that Hip Hop plays a role that the participant needed it to fill at the time. There are aesthetic- and leisure-related reasons that people are attracted to Hip Hop at an early age and it is not always the social message behind Hip Hop that is the reason (Osumare, 2005). It also seems that each participant was looking to Hip Hop to fulfill a specific role or void in their life at the time; understanding what that role or void was helps us to understand how each relates to Hip Hop culture individually. Thus, although the notion of a "Hip Hop generation" seemingly presents a monolithic entity with the same concerns, fears, and aspirations, this is not the case for these participants, each of whom came to and stayed with Hip Hop culture in his or her own way. I found that there were external factors such as familial influence, the aesthetic appeal of the style and sound, and the "cool" factor of Hip Hop that drew participants to initially enter Hip Hop culture. There were also internal factors such as participants seeking a way of expression and a community that solidified their engagement in Hip Hop and their art forms.

Jeffrey, a self-described emcee poet, was searching for a way to connect and express his blackness. Jeffrey is light-skinned, half

Scottish and half Badian and grew up in a mostly white city before he moved to Montreal. Before coming to Montreal, he spent much of his time with First Nations youth from the nearby reservation who were heavily influenced by a gangsta Hip Hop image cruising around in huge SUVs, blasting the latest West Coast single on their systems. Jeffrey's interview revealed that his decision to explore Hip Hop culture was just that—a decision. He consciously decided around the age of 16 to involve himself in a culture that would highlight his blackness. Jeffrey shared that, before Hip Hop, he dabbled in aggressive street skating and rock music, but always struggled with how to represent his black identity in a suburban community with only one other black family, in addition to his perception that people did not immediately "recognize" his blackness because of his lightness.

When he noticed that the Native youth were into Hip Hop, he saw a chance to explore his blackness, which he had not previously had many opportunities to express:

> Eloise: Why were you attracted to Hip Hop?
> Jeffrey: Well uh...before again it was identity. You know because I wanted to at one point like, race was a very important thing to me and I wanted to be more black (laughter).

Although Jeffrey attempts to brush off his concerns with his bi-racial background as a thing of the past, throughout the sessions and the interview, he often made reference to his struggles with finding a community he was comfortable with. At one point in the interview, he showed me two tattoos on the insides of his wrist where one is the outline of an empty circle and the other is a circle filled in black, and he explained: "Because it's my everything and nothing because it means, like, because my whole life is based off of black and white whether it be my mind and my body or whatever...I can always put it in that light of being split between two different things." He proceeds to share how even musically he feels split between the so-called white style of folk and the so-called black style of Hip Hop. Indeed, Jeffrey's mixing of folk and Hip Hop was challenged by others in the group because it was not Hip Hop. Interestingly, when other participants mixed reggae—a music entangled with blackness—with Hip Hop, they did not meet the same challenge that Jeffrey did.

Jeffrey seeks out ways to connect to the black community because he feels that his blackness is not apparent in his visual appearance as a light-skinned bi-racial person and he feels he has not had many "black" experiences in his life. As Johnson (2003) states, "The fact of blackness is not always self-constituting," (p. 2) and, as a result, members who feel on the periphery of the black community may search for ways to authenticate their blackness through performance and affiliation such as Jeffrey. While Jeffrey says offhandedly that he began listening to Hip Hop because he "wanted to be more black," he eventually came to align strongly with the theme of resistance within Hip Hop culture as he says, "But Hip Hop also forms like my attitude. Like I wrote a paper about civil disobedience and like you know I don't really like to take shit from people. I don't know, that's like…it's Hip Hop." Thus, we see how his position within Hip Hop progresses from an outsider-seeking authentication to someone who identifies with the culture's messages and ideology.

Blackness: You Got It or You Don't

The "it" in the above refers to Hip Hop credibility and authenticity. The following is an excerpt from a discussion that was the most cited discussion by participants throughout the sessions and into the interviews several months after it took place. Participants Ivan and Everson are at the centre of the debate, joined by another participant Eve, whose comments in French are translated into English. Ivan is a white Russian immigrant to Montreal, Everson is a black Haitian Brooklynite, and Eve is a black Congolese-French immigrant. Here we see the tensions between earning your place in the Hip Hop community through producing cultural artifacts such as graffiti and being granted a place in the Hip Hop community through being black. We were gathered as the larger group and our discussion began with the importance of involvement in the Hip Hop community. Ivan addressed Everson specifically among the group as a person who does not participate in any of the elements. Although there were four other people in the room who neither participate in any of the elements, Ivan spoke to Everson exclusively saying, "… you (addressing Everson) don't really have like a, like you're not really a Hip Hopper, you just enjoy Hip Hop. Right?" Everson immediately replied, "That's not what I said." The group discussion switched to a conversation between the two as Ivan rebutted: "Well, you don't do any of the elements right? You don't, you don't, and you don't freestyle. You don't break-dance. You don't really do any of the elements, am I right?" I noted that I was taken aback by Ivan's seemingly personal attack on Everson. Up until this point, group discussions were engaging, but never personal at this level. Everson's response to Ivan was full of emphasis and energy when he said, "Hip Hop is a culture! You don't have to do—." Ivan cut him off and continued, "A person who puts in work and who's been a rapper or who's been a graffiti writer. It's kind of; they're in a certain position to talk about it more than perhaps you. You know what I mean?" The rest of the group did not move to join their conversation. Everson replied, "I don't think that's true," and Ivan stood his ground, "I think it is."

Eve spoke up in French as she voiced support for Everson; translated[3], she said, "It's not cuz you dance or you do graffiti or you don't DJ or anyway that I take part in Hip Hop culture…it's not cuz I take my personal time to dance and that I spend 24 hours in a dance studio, I live Hip Hop but I live it in my own way, you get it? Everyone lives it in their own way." Ivan responded in French and, translated, said, "The person who creates, can talk about their element more because what he says has more weight." There was a palpable energy in the room where it seemed everyone wanted to address Ivan at once. Everson came out and said clearly to Ivan, "Well then, I have more weight than you because I'm black and you're not." Mayhem ensued. Everson's comment about being black seemed to take the participants by surprise and it was hard to decipher if people were supporting Everson or not since everyone was talking at the same time.

Although it was Everson's bringing up of race that ignited the discussion, the ensuing comments were remarkably sparse in their reference to race or blackness. The generic comment that was made by multiple participants was that: (a) we must recognize that Hip Hop is based upon black cultural forms and give credit where credit is due, and (b) as a culture, Hip Hop is diverse and welcoming of all ethnicities. The other black participants either did not address the issue or took the stance that race played no part in authenticity in Hip Hop. This silencing of race and of blackness specifically was remarkable given that the group rarely skirted around topics as blatantly as they did that day. Just as in Hill's (2009) classroom, race, blackness, and racism became unspoken realities throughout the Chronicle Creation sessions. I was surprised by this silencing because I thought that at the point of this discussion—almost two months into pre-production sessions—the group was developing into an open and safe space for critical discussion. Everson's comment momentarily uncovered racial tensions within the group and put on the table that as much as Ivan and others could "put in the work," there would always be something unknowable about Hip Hop culture to them because they were not black. Johnson (2003) expands upon this idea that there is more to blackness than performative acts:

> ...blackness is not always facilitated by performance. There are ways in which blackness exceeds the performative...blackness does not only reside in the theatrical fantasy of the white imaginary that is then projected onto black bodies, nor is it always consciously acted out; rather, it is also the inexpressible yet undeniable racial experience of black people—the ways in which the "living of blackness" becomes a material way of knowing. (p. 8)

Johnson puts forth that there is an essence to blackness in North America tied to the history of oppression and racialized experiences that continue to shape black lives today. His words support Everson's comment by asserting that there is some sort of essential quality to the black experience that must also be considered when one appropriates black cultures. Yet as Rose (2005) states, there is a way to honor the type of racialized knowledge Johnson speaks of, while also honoring the works of non-black folk in black cultures such as Hip Hop:

> Much ink has been spilled in the service of defending both the presumed fixity of blackness and the immovable parameters of black cultural boundaries...sustaining the category "black culture" does not require the denial of incorporation, hybridity, transformation and exchange....to acknowledge incorporation, transformation, change and hybridity in black culture does not bring an end to the category "black culture" or black people, for that matter. (p. viii)

Between Johnson (2003) and Rose (2005), it is evident that there was much to be explored and that was left unsaid during that group discussion on race. The scene mentioned above depicts how the group was not yet able to stray from the safe narrative of Hip Hop as an inclusive space and instead pull out the struggles each of them have with race and Hip Hop in their daily lives. Interestingly, the group's collective stance that race did not matter was not consistent with the individual interviews I conducted four months after the above scenario. While the group sessions were a public place for performing their status as Hip Hoppers, the interviews offered a kind of confessional setting to the participants as they divulged their attitudes towards the group sessions, the staff, and many of the same Hip Hop issues we spoke of in the group sessions.

The interviews reinforced my belief that that day the participants were not forthcoming with their issues of race and blackness. In all eight interviews, the notion of blackness as authentic in Hip Hop came up, unsolicited from me. For example, one participant, Prince, shared how he thought Hip Hop was a way to be black in Canada when he arrived from the Congo, Ivan shared how he and his friends "learned" most of their Hip Hop education from one of the black kids at school "who just knew" what was going on, Jeffrey sought out Hip Hop as a way to be more black as a bi-racial teen, and Benjamin shared how he has always felt the scrutiny of others in Hip Hop who see him as white and not Latino, which is an identity that is more easily accepted by Hip Hop in his eyes. Clearly, behind closed doors and away from the censorship of the group, Everson's statement about having more weight because he is black resonated with many of the other participants.

This discrepancy between the session and the interviews speaks to the advantage of being an insider and participant-observer within one's research community; in the interview, they were confiding in someone who had sat through the sessions with them and had built a personal relationship of trust and shared background in the documentary. As well, the discord between data from sessions and the interviews speaks to the ways in which interviews allow participants to directly tell their own stories about identity (Sfard and Prusak, 2005).

Conclusion: Placing Blackness and Masculinity in Hip Hop Culture

After taking a brief look at Jeffrey and Everson's relationships with blackness and Hip Hop culture, are we any more sure of how to locate young black men in Hip Hop? Perhaps the fact that we are unable to fix blackness in Hip Hop is the point: While we can be sure that Hip Hop culture will forever be entangled with blackness, we can never be sure of what shape or form that entanglement takes with each individual person. Blackness as an identity shifts and fluctuates for Jeffrey, Everson, and those that responded to Everson. If I approached Jeffrey five years from now and asked him the same question, "why Hip Hop?," perhaps his response will not have anything to do with blackness and identity. We are always in flux in relation to our various identities, at times working to reinforce an aspect—in Jeffrey's case, his blackness—while putting another in the background. However, as Gee asks, "What is at issue, though, is always how and by whom a particular identity is to be recognized" (p. 109). This statement is of particular interest when we consider the concept of authenticity and blackness in Hip Hop. If one has defined real-ness in Hip Hop as "being black"—such as Everson, then one fights against being recognized and affiliated with the negative stereotypes of black male identity construction in Hip Hop. The staff's reaction to Everson's statement about "being black" played an important role in shaping what the group accepted and rejected. From the beginning, the staff shared that they wanted to emphasize how Hip Hop was a culture that attracted and accepted all cultures. When the participants did not raise the theme of multiculturalism during an early session of brainstorming themes for the documentary, Marissa, one of the documentary producers, interjected and placed race, diversity, and multiculturalism on the table as the staff's sole contribution to the participant-generated list. Marissa had a clear commitment to exploring why Hip Hop attracts so many cultures, yet this was not shared by the group who actively steered conversation away from race, multiculturalism, and blackness.

Uncovering and speaking to those tensions instead of veering away from them could have been a mutually engaging learning process for the group.

Dolby's (2001) ethnographic work examining how students' taste preferences worked in tandem with their identity constructions speaks to the conscious and purposeful choices that participants make in consumption of music; she writes, "Youth use taste in conflicting ways: to reproduce their positions within racialized structures, and simultaneously to challenge those positions, cracking open spaces for the emergence of new identities, locations, and forms" (p. 67). Dolby's statement is especially relevant given that, after Hip Hop, the most popular music among the group was another black musical culture associated with resistance, reggae. From examining the various paths that led participants to Hip Hop, we can begin to see how their tastes cannot be solely explained away by Hip Hop's cool factor or aesthetic appeal. As Rose (2005) reminds, "We do not invest in cultures randomly; cultural exchanges, desires, appropriations, and affinities always speak to already existing relationships, conscious and otherwise—those we want to reinforce, transform, deny, embrace" (p.

viii). Indeed, with Jeffrey and Everson, there is no trace of "randomness" evident in why they chose and continue to choose Hip Hop. Jeffrey and Everson associated Hip Hop as encompassing more than just music and style; rather, they interpreted Hip Hop to be a culture, a way of life—a common answer to my question of what is Hip Hop was "Hip Hop is a way of thinking."

Notes

1. NFB funding ceased in 2009.
2. All 13 participants were contacted for interviews after pre-production. Only eight were available during the interview stage.
3. All translations were completed by the author.

References

Alim, H. S. (2004). *You know my steez: An ethnographic and sociolinguistic study of styleshifting in a black speech community.* Durham, NC: Duke University Press.

Brake, M. (1980). *The sociology of youth culture and youth subcultures: Sex and drugs and rock 'n' roll.* London: Routledge.

Brown, L., & Popplewell, B. (2008, January 30). Board okays black-focused school. The Toronto *Star*.

Chang, J. (2005). *Can't stop won't stop.* New York: Picador.

Dolby, N. (2001). *Constructing race: Youth identity, and popular culture in South Africa.* Albany: SUNY Press.

Forman, M. (2005). Straight outta Mogadishu: Prescribed identities and performative practices among Somali youth in North American high schools. In S. Maira & E. Soep (Eds.), *Youthscapes: The popular, the national, the global*(pp.3-22). Philadelphia: University of Pennsylvania Press.

Gee, J. (2000). Identity as an analytic lens for research in education. *Review of Research in Education 25*, 99-125.

Ginwright, S. (2004). *Black in school: Afrocentric reform, urban youth, and the promise of Hip Hop culture.* New York: Teachers College Press.

Hill, M. L. (2009). *Beats, rhymes, and classroom life: Hip Hop pedagogy and the politics of identity.* New York: Teachers College Press.

Hollands, R. (2001). (Re)presenting Canadian youth: Challenge or opportunity. In M. Gauthier & D. Pacom (Eds.), *Spotlight on Canadian youth research*(pp.99-117). Saint Nicolas: Les Presses De L'Universite Laval.

Ibrahim, A. (1999). Becoming black: Rap and Hip Hop, race, gender, identity, and the politics of ESL learning. *TESOL Quarterly 33*(3), 349–369.

Ibrahim, A. (2004). Operation under erasure: Hip Hop and the pedagogy of affective. *Journal of Curriculum Theorizing 20,* 113–133.

Johnson, P. (2003). *Appropriating blackness: Performance and the politics of authenticity.* Durham: Duke University Press.

Kelly, J. (2007). Diasporan moves: African Canadian youth and identity formation. In N. Dolby & F. Rizvi (Eds.), *Youth moves: Identities and education in global perspective* (pp.85-100). London: Routledge.

Low, B., Tan, E., & Celemencki. (forthcoming) Authenticity and identity in community learning spaces. In *Schooling in Hip Hop: New approaches to hip hop education.* New York: Teachers College Press.

Osumare, H. (2005). Global Hip Hop and the African diaspora. In H. J. Elam Jr. & K. Jackson (Eds.), *Black cultural traffic: Crossroads in global performance and popular culture* (pp.266-288). Ann Arbor, MI: University of Michigan Press.

Rose, T. (2005). Foreword. In H. Elam Jr. & K. Jackson (Eds.), *Black cultural traffic: Crossroads in global performance and popular culture*(pp.vii-viii). Ann Arbor, MI: University of Michigan Press.

Rose, T. (2008). *The Hip Hop wars.* New York: Basic Books.

Sackeyfio, C. N. T. (2006). Hip Hop cultural identities: A review of the literature and its implication for the schooling of African-Canadian youth (Masters thesis, University of Toronto, 2006). Masters Abstracts International, 44, 06.

Sarkar, M., & L. Winer. (2006). Multilingual code-switching in Quebec rap: Poetry, pragmatics and performativity. *International Journal of Multilingualism 3*(3), 173-192.

Sarkar, M., & D. Allen. (2007). Identity in Quebec Hip Hop: Language, territory and ethnicity in the mix. *Journal of Language, Identity and Education 6*(2), 117-130.

Sfard, A., & Prusak, A. (2005). Telling identities: In search of an analytic tool for investigating learning as a culturally shaped activity. *Educational Researcher 34*(4), 14-22.

Tan, E. (2009). Participatory and critical out-of-school learning for urban youth: Building community through popular culture. Unpublished dissertation. McGill University, Montreal.

Tsolidis, G. (2006). *Youthful imagination: Schooling, subcultures, and social justice.* New York: Peter Lang.

Yon, D. (2000). *Elusive culture: Schooling, race, and identity in global times.* New York: SUNY.

Biography

Eloise Tan, Ph.D., is a researcher, scholar, and community worker. She has worked with urban youth community programs in Montreal and Toronto ranging from after-school Hip Hop programs to anti-racist training for students. Eloise is currently based in Dublin, Ireland at Dublin City University.

Reframing Black Male Homosociality as Critical Spaces to Explore Black Masculinity

Anthony R. Keith, Jr.

The Pennsylvania State University

Abstract

Black masculinity was examined within the context of sites where public platonic practices of affection amongst Black men are evident. An overview of the limited scholarship and research on Black male homosocial experiences within sports, hip-hop culture, the Black church, Black barbershops, and Black fraternities were explored. An argument for using art as an abstract space to further the study of homosocial relationships amongst Black men was provided; the author referenced his own creative writing throughout the article as an example. The conclusion suggests scholars and researchers interested in studying Black masculinity can serve as agents of change on this issue by framing their analysis around positive and public practices of love for and amongst Black men.

NOTE: An original poem composed by the author is woven throughout the article. The full poem is provided in the Appendix section.

"words have power / letters are electrically charged / and when bounded together /
they can create enough energy / to cause a massive explosion / words can turn tiny mountain tops / in to mighty metaphorical

erosions / and it will be I / who stands atop one of those mounds / with words / vowels / syllables / phrases / and sounds/ and I'll be screaming / THIS IS FOR ALL OF YA'LL STILL DREAMING! /"

bell hooks provides an unequivocally strong argument for men to critique patriarchy and involve themselves in shaping feminist movement and addressing male liberation in her 2004 book, *We Real Cool: Black Men and Masculinity*. She expresses a hope that "Black men who care about the plight of Black males and who are themselves advocates of feminist thinking would do more to reach out to Black males as a group" (p. xvi). So far, as she continues to state, "that work has not been forthcoming." Similar to Neal's (2005) reflection on his feminist identity development, I too acknowledge my inability to critically examine and write about Black gender ideologies until challenged by a Black woman. I felt like she was directly challenging me to take action, or continue to be a Black man who contributes to the widening gap in scholarship about Black masculinity. Therefore, as both a Black man and a feminist, I feel compelled to probe the critical spaces that shape Black masculinity and seek to help close the gap.

Roberts's (1994) analysis of Black male relationships indicates there is very little scholarly research that explores healthy and constructive relationships among African American boys and men. In particular, Roberts argues that there is a need for a more Afrocentric approach to studying Black masculinity that would examine how males relate to each other. The European models often used by researchers and theorists place men in opposition with each other; the African model, on the other hand, stresses the importance of communal needs and interconnectedness. Most scholarly works on the topic of Black masculinity often examine the Black male experience within larger social context like hip hop, media, politics, and education. Rarely, however, are the experiences amongst Black men within those social contexts explored. Therefore, an examination of the physical and emotional practice of authentic love for and amongst Black men is not only a scholarship inquiry, but a pragmatic necessity. Black men need to understand, feel, and practice an ethic of love for each other that fosters a healthy masculinity. However, this becomes a challenge when Black masculinity is confined to White, American patriarchal structures that are rooted in homophobia. Black men must negotiate their love for each other in a society that not only demonizes and hates them, but stigmatizes Black gay and bisexual men. hooks (2005) states "Black men are not loved by White men, White women, Black women, or girls and boys. And that especially most black men do not love themselves" (p. xi). Scholars and researchers interested in studying Black masculinity can serve as agents of change on this issue by framing their analysis around positive and public practices of love amongst Black men.

The status of Black men in America is a publicly discussed phenomenon that often limits its discourse to statics on high incarceration rates, low educational attainment, and family abandonment. As Neal explains in his (2005) book, *The New Black Man*, the "Black Man in Crisis" is the theme of hundreds of newspaper, magazine, and journal articles and·conferences over the last twenty years. According to Neal, the influx of public messages about Black men has perhaps made it easy to "isolate the Tupac Shakurs, Allen Iversons, 'Pookies,' and Nushawn Williamses of the world and make them the reason why the black man has failed (p.3)." I question the ability of Black men to express legitimate public acts of love amongst each other, while simultaneously internalizing public attacks on their race and gender identities. This double consciousness, according to Collins (2005), has ascribed a new identity for Black men as the "Endangered Black Male," or a Black man with untapped potential who will never reach his dreams due to internalized oppression fostered by these statics. In 2008, CNN presented the plight of Black men as a segmented topic in one of their "Black in America" special reports. I imagine that Black men are significantly underrepresented in the CNN viewer demographic and thus, question the targeted audience for these special reports. Publicly acknowledging Black men as a species worth investigation is not only pejorative, malicious, and dehumanizing, but it further perpetuates a philosophy that Black men are unlovable.

"those of you / whose hue / starts of as black / until you've been beaten down to blue /

don't know who the fuck you are / because you're letting society define it for you/

aint got a pot to piss in / or a window to throw it out of / and no food to chew /

and so you're starving / starving for knowledge/ not because you don't grasp the language / but because no one took the time to teach it to you /"

I became interested in this topic after several accounts of both observing and participating in public practices of platonic affection amongst men in Tanzania. I participated in a cultural immersion program in Tanzania as a graduate student in 2006 and two additional experiences as a cultural practitioner in higher education from 2009 to 2010. Each visit lasted between three to five weeks and included field studies that focused on gender development and artistic culture in dominant and indigenous communities. Although the studies were primarily exploring the experiences of women, I could not help but to observe the relationships amongst Tanzanian men. I observed them holding hands together while strolling through villages and cities, sleeping up to five men in the same bed, leaning on each other during moments of rest, and dancing and singing with each other in night clubs and during cultural celebrations. I soon learned that being in close proximity with and showing love for other men in Tanzania was a performance of masculinity. Perhaps there is no visible threat to masculinity within this context because homosexuality is illegal in the country. Therefore, any public identification or practice that the law constitutes as homosexual would be met with significantly negative repercussions.

Each time I returned back to the United States, I had to adjust my gender performance to adhere to socially accepted patterns of Black masculinity. In other words, public displays of platonic affection are confined to half-handshake-half-hugs and maintaining a spatial territory between myself and other Black men. Certainly, the historical constructs of race, ethnicity, gender, and sexuality that shape Black masculinity in the United States are a flawed comparison to that of Tanzanian men. However, I am interested in examining practices of love amongst Black men in the United States with regard to segregated gender spaces. Like Neal (2005) advocates, I want to serve as a champion of a movement where Black men are not homophobes. I seek to not only challenge social barriers that frame Black masculinity, but foster an authentic love amongst Black men regardless of their intersecting identities.

> "but brothers / I have something more empowering to tell you/ even if the world doesn't / please know that I LOVE YOU /
> and I love you / with all of the African ancestry that exist within me/ from my forehead /
> to my collar bone / from my bloodstream / to my skin tone / from my strong back /
> to my humble knees / from my shinbone / to my callused feet /
> and brothers / I DECLARE YOU FREE! /"

Therefore, this article will explore Black male homosocial spaces and public practices of love, as well as present an argument that art, as an abstract space, can be used as an additional lens for exploring Black masculinity.

I acknowledge that Black men are not a homogenous group, and their identities and experiences vary greatly. Therefore, my discussion of love amongst Black men is not intended for generalist applications. It is my hope, however, to encourage critical dialogue on Black male gender performances and develop strategies that challenge controlled images of Black masculinity. In an effort to distinguish homosocial from homosexual within this article, I will intermittently refer to platonic practices of love and affection amongst Black men. Also, the terms African-American and Black will be used interchangeably to reflect terminology used within scholarship and research on this topic.

The Journal of Black Masculinity, Vol. 1, No. 1, Fall 2010

Sports: A Homosocial Space Controlled by Violence and Competition

"they just told you that you're too stubborn to listen to /
that your head's too thick to get a brick through / that you're
nothing / but a no-good /
pants-sagging / baby-making / law-breaking / violent / juvenile
delinquent / that all you're capable to do / is simply eat / sleep /
shit / and screw / "

It is usually within the context of athletic competition and braggadocio that Black men are permitted to show any forms of affection towards each other that is void of eroticism. Unfortunately, these acts of affection are rooted in a history of violence and Black male domination by White American patriarchy. Ferber (2007) argues that key elements of White supremacy and the new racism are reinforced by popular representations of Black male athletes. Ferber explored contemporary illustrations of Black males as violent and hypersexual. Using recent examples of violence by African American professional sports players such as Kobe Bryant, O.J. Simpson, and Mike Tyson, Ferber pivots themes of Black masculinity around White patriarchal gender ideologies. Missing from Ferber's analysis however, is an examination of the relationships that exist within Black male athlete groups.

Boxing, for example, is a sport that permits Black men to fight, then kiss and make up. In May 2010, after twelve rounds of brutally beating each other, professional boxers, Floyd Mayweather and Shane Mosley, embraced each other and exchanged words of endearment. Publicly admitting that they loved each other was not only a sign of good sportsmanship, it was also an example Black men reinforcing a controlled masculinity. Prior to the boxing match, the two verbally attacked each other in an artful display of words and gestures aimed at de-masculinization. Pounding their fists and calling each other "sissies", "soft," and "punks," were undoubtedly attempts to confirm to traditionally masculine ideals. However, after the match, they were able to negotiate a homosocial space where platonic love is controlled by violence and competition.

As Hill (2005) suggests in his article on subverting traditional masculinity, Black men are permitted to express love on the basketball court by giving high-fives, chest bumps, and ass smacks. He identifies the basketball court as a space for "offering the type of caring touches, kind words, and genuine regard for other brothers that most of us possess but aren't permitted to share except under very limited and heavily surveyed conditions" (para. 1). Tucker's (2003) analysis of representations of Black male athletes suggests that given the images of an emotional, loving community of Black men does not accord with hegemonic images of aggressive Black men whose sole purposes in life are to destroy self and community. "The most frightening symbol, for White people, is Black men in love. The moment Black men love each other, the United States is done for" (Tucker, 2003, p. 313).

Hall (2001), on the other hand, critiqued the overrepresentation of Black men in a professional sports industry that is both controlled and admired by White Americans. Hall provides a critical analysis of Black masculinity within the historical context of White voyeurism on Black male bodies. In particular, Hall posits White American's fascination of Black male athletic talent is rooted in longstanding beliefs that Black men's bodies are biologically suited for superior athleticism, yet they are intellectually inferior to their White counterparts. Missing from Hall's critique, however, is an exploration of the interpersonal relationships amongst Black male athletes that mutually shape Black masculinity. If Black men are overrepresented in sports, then how do they negotiate their relationships with each other?

Hip Hop: A Homosocial Space Controlled by Hypermasculinity

"so fuck / being afraid to use slang / because I'm granting you the right / to use the language of your people / to move the masses /"

Black male homosocial experiences are also present in hip hop culture. After a lyrical analysis of 478 songs by top record selling Black rap artists, Oware (2010) concluded that most homosocial content is confined within three major themes: 1) rappers defining their male friends as family members; 2) rappers utilizing their personal achievements for the benefit of their male friends; and 3) lamenting the incarceration or death of a companion. As an example, Oware provides an excerpt from Jay-Z's "Do You Wanna Ride" from his album *Kingdom Come* (2007):

I said 'we' cause I'm here, you here!/
Yeah, ride with me, your spot is reserved family/
cigarette boats, yachts, ain't nowhere we can't go/
We in South Beach and the Hamptons too baby/

Complimenting these lyrical themes are music videos that portray groups of Black men engaging in platonic, yet affectionate masculine performances. I am still fascinated when I see rapper Ron Browz spraying and pouring champagne on some his Black male comrades in his "Pop Champagne" video; this is justified, however, through extremely misogynistic lyrics. Neal (2005) states that Black men in hip hop videos are performing their notions of how American masculinity embodies power through force, violence, and exploitation. Hill (2009) suggests, despite Hip Hop's explicitly homophobic message dissemination, there are strong attempts by rap artist to justify the contradictory homoerotic behaviors. According to Hill (2009), "rap artist have even deployed homophobic slang like 'pause' and 'no homo' after uttering words that could be (mis)construed as homoerotic in order to preemptively defend themselves against allegations of homosexuality" (p. 32).

Black Church: A Homosocial Space Controlled by Emotional Vulnerability

"I'm holding ya'll up on my shoulders / giving ya'll a higher view /
I'm breaking ya'll through mountain tops / and wading through muddy waters /
and don't worry / because historically / I've been know to split that shit in two/"

My father is a minister and an evangelist for a predominately Black church in Washington, D.C. He is responsible for meeting the faith-based needs of his church community and also providing service and support for the church's Bishop, a Black male. Recently, my father told me that he "loves" his Bishop and that he embraces that man as not only his spiritual leader but as a father, friend, and confidant. His use of the word "love" sparked my inquisition of Black churches as safely controlled spaces that foster platonic love for and amongst Black men.

Ward (2005) explores the relationship between theologically driven homophobia and anti-homosexual rhetoric of Black Nationalism in Black churches. Framing homophobia as a pillar of hegemonic masculinity, Ward argues homophobia is used as a strategy of domination to define not only who is homosexual, but who is not a man. Additionally, he posits church-related homophobia influences conceptions of what is to be a Black man, thereby influencing the behavior and lives of Black males. While Ward's (2005) article provides a rich analysis of the significance of the Black church on shaping heterosexual hypermasculinity, it fails to address the platonic relationships amongst men in the Black church. I have personally participated and observed Black men in church crying, physically embracing, praying, and affectionately worshiping with each other—all forms of a vulnerable masculinity. Although confined to the walls of churches and other places of faith, Black men negotiate these spaces as safe locations to express their love for God and for each other.

Black Barbershops: A Homosocial Space Controlled by Cultural Exchanges

"but brothers / I have something more empowering to tell you/ even if the world doesn't please know that I LOVE YOU /

Black barbershops are cultural spaces that thrive on homosocial experiences amongst Black men. This is one of the few spaces where the physical presence of women is virtually non-existent. One of my female friends maintains a short haircut and asked if I would accompany her to a Black barbershop in her neighborhood. When I asked why she needed me, she indicated that it was a place where Black men go to be with each other and, unless accompanied by a man, women are not welcomed. I wondered what she thought took place in such a segregated gender space. I informed her that there is no secret code of behavior, but there is an underlying message that permits platonic practices of affection amongst Black men.

Alexander's (2003) interpretive indigenous ethnographic study of black barbershops as cultural spaces included accounts of unacknowledged yet sanctioned intimate contact amongst other men.

Luke leans his body against mine when he is trimming my facial hair. I am not sexualizing Luke or the experience, for he is a father figure.

> We understand the meaningfulness of the
> engagement, not only the functionality of the
> action but in the knowing. The knowing—that a
> Black man who knows and understands the
> growth pattern of Black hair and the sensitivity
> of Black skin—is caring for another Black man.
> (p. 120)

I too experience similar acts of love when I visit my barbershop back home. Even in a space dominated by Black men, it is acceptable for my barber to publicly announce how much he has missed me since my last visit and tell me he loves me when I leave. We give each other full embraces, smiles, and engage in playful banter with other Black men in the shop. Sometimes we converse about sports and pop culture; other times we have more intimate dialogue about family troubles and romantic relationships. According to Alexander (2003), unlike stoic images of Black masculinity expressed in media and pop culture, barbershops are cultural sites where Black men engage in friendly exchanges, all-the-while, negotiating space and intention.

Fraternities: A Homosocial Space Controlled by Brotherhood

"so brothers / if I have to fight your battles/ and brothers / if I have to take your blows /
don't you worry / because I will do it for you / I will do it / "

African American fraternities serve as another site for examining homosocial experiences of Black men. I come across countless photos on Facebook of Black fraternity men joined together to form a "line;" they are positioned chest-to-back with their arms folded underneath one another, and they are basically holding each other as close as possible. These photos are public and often have captions like "I love my LB (line brother)."

However, I have also witnessed some of the same fraternity men refusing to sleep in the same bed at a leadership conference.

Harper and Harris (2006) analysis on the role of Black fraternities conclude racial identity, leadership development, cognitive development and practical competence are positive outcomes on African American college males. There is very little discussion, however, in their study on the positive relationships amongst fraternity members. The researchers did provide some indication that fraternity members in their study mentioned "having a life long expectation of service to the organization and unconditional support to each other" (p. 133).

Similarly, results from McClure's (2006) study of twenty members of a historically Black fraternity at a large predominately White institution concluded that cooperation and community building was a common thematic construct of masculinity. McClure suggests a cooperative feeling also sets up the possibility for more honest and authentic relationships among men. "They are no longer in competition with one another and the fraternity often provided the members with their first opportunity to experience 'real,' emotionally honest relationships with men" (p. 66). Kiesling's (2005) study concluded homosociality is performed "indirectly" or with "disclaimers," amongst fraternity men, but it is nevertheless central to the men's social identities, especially as fraternity members. However, Kiesling's participants were members of a predominately White fraternity, which leaves little to the cultural discourse on Black male fraternity members. An in-depth exploration of the positive outcomes of brotherhood on Black masculinity and its relationship to fraternity membership is sorely needed.

Art: An Unrestricted Homosocial Space

"I will do it / and I will smile / I will do it/ with a heart as pure as the metaphors / in the poems of Langston Hughes / and as cool / as the vibrato in B.B. King's blues /"

It is clear that research on the topic of public platonic practices of love amongst Black men is missing within research and scholarship on the topic of Black masculinity. Art is an additional homosocial space lacking attention, yet worthy of exploration. Art can function as an abstract, inclusive, homosocial space that promotes authentic love for and amongst Black men. Most creative art forms do not have to conform to social institutions, rubrics, and standards. Spoken word poetry, for example, is an artistic performance in which individualism is encouraged and words and messages can vary in style, tone, and texture. I think it would behoove Black men to embrace masculinity like art; one that is void of social restrictions, but guided by introspection and most importantly, with love.

While researching information to frame the concepts of this article, I came across a Wikipedia entry on the Mythopoetic Men's Movement (2010). This social movement began around the early 1980's and consists of a body of organized work that seeks to foster healthy psychosocial development amongst men. One of the tenets of this movement includes a focus on engaging men's exegesis through personal narratives, story telling, poetry, and other literary and performance arts as tools for introspection. In other words, help men understand themselves as men in artistic ways that promote emotional and psychological development.

As a feminist, I am critical of how a movement to foster male identity development can be utilized as an advocacy tool for women's rights all over the world. However, as a spoken word artist and poet, I can identify with the importance of using the power of words and language in artistic spaces that promote social justice.

According to Collins (2005), loving Black people (as distinguished from dating/or having sex with Black people) in a society that is so dependent on hating Blackness constitutes a highly rebellious act. Therefore, I referenced pieces of my own literary work throughout this article not only as an act of rebellion, but also as a public declaration of authentic love for myself and for all of the other Black men.

Discussion

It is my hope that other Black male feminists, scholars, educators, artist and writers who love Black men continue to contribute to a new framework for examining Black masculinity. Researchers and scholars, I implore you to dedicate time and effort to examine the positive relationships amongst Black men that foster a healthy masculinity. By focusing on gender constructs that contradict cultural norms and values on the Black male experience, we can shape a new framework that positively examines Black masculinity. Artists, I am advocating that you create pieces dedicated to Black male platonic practices of love. Utilizing an abstract space that lacks boundaries and constrictions can not only be creatively liberating, but socially liberating for those Black men in bondage. Educators, I am asking that you use the artwork and the research as pedagogical tools to foster global learning and engagement with issues of Black masculinity. Challenge your students to engage in critical and reflective dialogue on the content put forth by artist, researchers, and scholars.

"we fight with one fist in the air / but with me beside you / we now fight / with the power of two / and until / you have gained the wisdom / and until / you have learned how to work the system / and until / you can walk / with your footsteps / next to

mine / don't you worry brothers / I will continue to carry you /
as long as you remember / to pick up /
and carry those that are left behind /"

References

Alexander, B. K. (2003). Fading, twisting, and weaving: An interpretive ethnography of the Black barbershop as cultural space. *Qualitative Inquiry, 9*(1), 105-128.

Collins, P. H. (2005). *Black sexual politics: African Americans, gender, and the new racism.* New York: Routledge.

Ferber, A. L. (2007). The construction of Black masculinity: White supremacy now and then. *Journal of Sport & Social Issues, 31*(11), 11-24.

Hall, R. E. (2001). The ball curve calculated racism and the stereotype of African American men. *Journal of Black Studies, 32*(1), 104-119.

Harper, S. R., & Harris, F. (2006). The role of Black fraternities in the African American male undergraduate experience. In M. J. Cuyjet (Author), *African American men in college* (pp. 128-153). San Francisco: Jossey-Bass.

Hill, M. L. (2005, November 04). Breaking the rules: Subverting traditional masculinity on the court and beyond. *Seeingblack.com.* Retrieved May 06, 2010, from http://www.seeingblack.com/2005/x110405/bball.shtml

Hill, M. L. (2009). Scared straight: Hip-hop, outing, and the pedagogy of queerness. *Review of Education, Pedagogy, and Cultural Studies, 31*(1), 29-54.

hooks, b. (2004). *We real cool: Black men and masculinity.* New York: Routledge.

Kiesling, S. F. (2005). Homosocial desire in men's talk: Balancing and re-creating cultural. *Language in Society, 34*(5).

McClure, S. M. (2006). Improvising masculinity: African American fraternity membership in the construction of Black masculinity. *Journal of African American Studies, 10*(1), 57-73.

Mythopoetic men's movement. (n.d.). Wikipedia, the free encyclopedia. Retrieved June 11, 2010,
from
http://en.wikipedia.org/wiki/Mythopoetic_men's_movement

Neal, M. A. (2005). *New Black man.* New York: Routledge.

Oware, M. (2010). Brotherly Love: Homosociality and Black masculinity in gangsta rap music. *Journal of African American Studies.* doi: 10.1007/s12111-010-9123-4

Roberts, G. W. (1994). Brother to brother: African American modes of relating among men. *Journal of Black Studies, 24*(4), 379-390.

Tucker, L. (2003). Blackballed: Basketball and representations of the Black male athlete. *American Behavioral Scientist, 47*(3), 306-328.

Ward, E. G. (2005). Homophobia, hypermasculinity and the US Black church. *Culture, Health & Sexuality, 7*(5), 493-504.

Biography

Anthony R. Keith, Jr. served as the Interim Director of the Paul Robeson Cultural Center and an Instructor in African American Studies at The Pennsylvania State University, where he earned his master's degree in College Student Affairs. He is currently the Coordinator for Cultural Competency & Diversity for the Fall 2010 Voyage of Semester at Sea. Correspondence concerning this article should be addressed to Anthony R. Keith, Jr., 3100 Metronome Turn, Clinton MD 20735
Email: arkeithjr@gmail.com

Appendix

A Poem for Black Men by Anthony Keith

1. words have power / letters are electrically charged / and when bounded together / they can create enough energy / to cause a massive explosion /
2. words can turn tiny mountain tops / in to mighty metaphorical erosions / and it will be I / who stands atop one of those mounds / with words / vowels / syllables / phrases / and sounds/ and I'll be screaming /
3. THIS IS FOR ALL OF YA'LL STILL DREAMING! /
4. those of you / whose hue / starts of as black / until you've been beaten down to blue /
5. don't know who the fuck you are / because you're letting society define it for you/
6. aint got a pot to piss in / or a window to throw it out of / and no food to chew /
7. and so you're starving / starving for knowledge/ not because you don't grasp the language /
8. but because no one took the time to teach it to you /
9. they just told you that you're too stubborn to listen to /
10. that your head's too thick to get a brick through / that you're nothing / but a no-good /
11. pants-sagging / baby-making / law-breaking /juvenile delinquent / that all you're capable to do / is simply eat / sleep / shit / and screw /
12. but brothers / I have something more empowering to tell you/ even if the world doesn't
13. please know that I LOVE YOU /

14. and I love you / with all of the African ancestry that exist within me/ from my forehead /

15. to my collar bone / from my bloodstream / to my skin tone / from my strong back /

16. to my humble knees / from my shinbone / to my callused feet /

17. and brothers / I DECLARE YOU FREE! /

18. no longer / property/ no longer / a weapon for society / to continue to arm you /

19. with massive missiles / of misguide perceptions / of manhood / in to your looking glasses

20. so fuck / sitting in the back / writing "R.I.P" to your friends on that dirty desk/ you're now in the front / teaching classes /

21. so fuck / being afraid to use slang / because I'm granting you the right / to use the language of your people / to move the masses /

22. and fuck / waiting in the back of the line / just to get to the front / I'm giving you a lifetime supply of free V.I.P. backstage passes/

23. and if someone said you didn't pay your way / tell them fuck you / cause its already being deducted from your taxes / and if they say they need proof /

24. tell them they can find it / printed on paychecks / made from trees / that were once used / to whip the back of slave's asses /

25. and if they still have questions / tell them / I can call up the Black men's headquarters /

26. and have them send that shit out through smoke signals / or morse code dashes /

27. and if they still have questions / tell them / they can take a pin / and prick your skin /

28. and check your deoxyribonucleic acid / better known as your D.N.A. /

29. they Don't Need Answers / they Don't Need Anything / and if they claim they do /

30. you can tell them to come and see me / because I GOT YOU /

31. I'm holding ya'll up on my shoulders / giving ya'll a higher view /

32. I'm breaking ya'll through mountain tops / and wading through muddy waters /
33. and don't worry / because historically / I've been know to split that shit in two/
34. so brothers / if I have to fight your battles/ and brothers / if I have to take your blows /
35. don't you worry / because I will do it for you /
36. I will do it / and I will smile /
37. I will do it/ with a heart as pure as the metaphors / in the poems of Langston Hughes /
38. and as cool / as the vibrato in B.B. King's blues /
39. and I'll do it / while wearing a black hat / black shirt / black tie / black pants / black draws / black socks / and a cool ass pair of motherfucking of black suede shoes /
40. I might even do it / as an interruption / of the morning news /
41. but instead / I'll be screaming / NEWS FLASH! / NEWS FLASH! /
42. Black men America is trying to take your freedom / but they can't take the rest of you /
43. they claim / they got you by the balls / but lets face it / you're a Black man / and they have small hands /
44. so stereotypically they can barely / grip one of your testicles /
45. tell them / they need to step their game up /
46. take some vitamin B / or eat some more vegetables /
47. but no matter / what they try to do / they will never / ever / be stronger / than you /
48. we fight with one fist in the air / but with me beside you / we now fight / with the power of two /
49. and until / you have gained the wisdom /
50. and until / you have learned how to work the system /
51. and until / you can walk / with your footsteps / next to mine /
52. don't you worry brothers /
53. I will continue to carry you /
54. as long as you remember / to pick up /and carry those that are left behind

Walk Like a Man, Talk Like a Man: Examining Masculinity and Femininity in Gay Black Men on the Cable Television Show *Noah's Arc*

Alfred Martin

The University of Texas at Austin

Abstract

This study examines masculinity and stereotypes of gay black men as they are presented on the cable television series Noah's Arc, *a show that follows the lives and loves of four gay black men in Los Angeles. The nine, approximately 30-minute episodes that constitute the first season of* Noah's Arc *were analyzed for content and coded based on attributes most associated with male homosexuals and male heterosexuals as found in Mary Kite and Kay Deaux's study on gender belief systems (1987). Once coded, the data were analyzed to determine the prevalence of stereotypical masculine and feminine characteristics and/or behaviors. An analysis was conducted to examine the characters, their constructions, and the way gay black masculinity is perceived and disseminated on the show.*

Introduction

Given that television is the primary source of information and socialization in the United States (Bryant & Zillman, 1986), it is no wonder that much research has been devoted to the way in which television portrays various groups of people on television. There has been research on the way black people are portrayed on television (Berry, 1980; Payne, 1994; and Ward, 2004) and the way in which gay people are portrayed on television (Fouts & Inch, 2005; Raley & Lucas, 2006; and Fisher, Hill & Gruber, 2007), but the point at which blackness and homosexuality intersect on television has not been researched.

In 2005, LOGO, a cable television network targeting gay, lesbian, bisexual and transgender viewers, announced that it would debut *Noah's Arc*, a series chronicling the lives of four Los Angeles-based gay black men. The creator of *Noah's Arc* developed the show because he perceived a lack of gay black characters on popular television shows such as *Queer as Folk* and *Will & Grace* (Odenwald, 2004). With few exceptions—including Antoine Merriweather and Blaine Edwards on *In Living Color*, Carter Heywood on *Spin City*, Dr. Dennis Hancock on *Chicago Hope* and Keith Charles on *Six Feet Under*—gay black men had been largely invisible on television.

Noah's Arc, according its website, is marketed as an exploration

> of the lives and loves of four African-American gay men looking for love and signs of intelligent life in West Hollywood. This one-of-a-kind groundbreaking original series tells the story of Noah, Chance, Alex, and Ricky as they deal with boyfriends, struggle to build careers and search for Mr. Right. It's Sex and the Citymeets Soul Food—but gay, of course.

For gay black men, this show could serve as a "looking glass self" moment with their image (or at least an image) reflected back to them from the television screen. The show had its fair share of supporters and detractors with some believing that the show revisits old stereotypes of gay men and others, and others heralding the show for its representations of gay black men. These diametrically opposed positions about *Noah's Arc* are the driving forces behind the current study. The research questions that drive this project are: How are stereotypes of gay men utilized in the construction of the characters on *Noah's Arc*? How does the show construct masculinity and femininity? Why do (or should) we care about the way in which stereotypes and notions of a masculinity/femininity binary within homosexual relationships are deployed in portrayals of gay black men on *Noah's Arc*?

As someone who is male, black and gay, my interest in the show stemmed from a desire to see myself reflected on the television screen in what I perceived as a vacuum of representation of gay black men on television—network or cable. *Noah's Arc* was the first time that a television series focused solely on gay black men dealing seriously with both friendships and sexual/romantic relationships and, while ground-breaking, it is important to look critically at the show to examine how these gay black men are portrayed.

A Brief Televisual History of Gay Black Men

While the first "queer" character appeared on television in 1953 on the sitcom *Private Secretary*, the first explicitly gay black male characters didn't appear on primetime network television until 1990 on FOX's sketch comedy show, *In Living Color*, with the characters Antoine Merriweather (David Alan Grier) and Blaine Edwards (Damon Wayans). While some in the gay community have taken and continue to take issue with what they deem the stereotypical portrayal of gay black men on the show generally and the "Men On..." sketches specifically, the appearance of gay black men on network television moved the group from non-representation or invisibility to Cedric Clark's (1969) second stage of minority representation on television: Ridicule. What is important about the move from invisibility to visibility is that television is often seen as a way to validate one's existence. In other words, if you're on television, you exist. But as gay black men moved from invisibility, they moved to being the object of derisive humor, as outlined in Clark's stages of representation. While gay black men were no longer invisible to television audiences, they were being ridiculed and positioned on the receiving end of jokes.

That same year, another portrayal of a gay black man could be found on FOX's sitcom *Roc*. Interestingly, the gay character Russell was played by actor Richard Roundtree, best known for his portrayal of Shaft in the 1970s blaxploitation film of the same name. Richard Roundtree playing this role is important intertextually. Many in the audience remembered Roundtree in the role of Shaft, a hypersexual, heterosexual black action hero. As such, many may have brought that understanding of Roundtree to his role in *Roc*, which would have added to the audience's surprise when his character comes out as a gay man.

No other gay black male characters appeared on television until 1996. This was also the year Ellen DeGeneres's character on *Ellen* came out of the closet, becoming the first gay or lesbian lead character on television. On *Spin City*, Michael Boatman's character Carter Heywood became the first gay black male character to co-star on a network television show. In the 1997-98 television season, in addition to Carter Heywood, *Chicago Hope* added Dr. Dennis Hancock, a gay black man portrayed by Vondie Curtis-Hall. These two portrayals were the only representations of gay black men on network television for the 1998-1999 and 1999-2000 television seasons.

In the 2000-2001 and 2001-2002 seasons, Carter Heywood remained the only gay black male character on network television. However, there was one gay black male character on cable television on HBO's *Six Feet Under*, Keith Charles, played by Matthew St. Patrick. In addition, in the 2001-2002 season, HBO's *The Wire* featured as a recurring character a gay black man, Omar Little, played by actor Michael K. Williams. The following year, there were no gay black men on network television, as *Spin City* was cancelled. Keith Charles and Omar Little were the two gay black characters on cable television during the 2002-2003 and 2003-2004 television seasons.

During the 2004-2005 season, a new show, *Eyes*, featured a gay black man, although his appearance was short-lived as the show lasted less than a season. In addition, Julien, a gay black male, appeared on the FX show *The Shield*. The following year, the short-lived ABC show (only one episode aired before being cancelled) *Emily's Reasons Why*

Not introduced a gay black male character, Josh, and *Noah's Arc*, the show on which this study is based, premiered on cable television during this season and featured four gay black male lead characters as well as several gay black male supporting characters.

Stereotypes: Positive, Negative, or…?

A brief discussion of stereotypes is important here. Walter Lippman (1922) argued that stereotypes play an important role in human judgment and information processing. (p. 4) Television has the power to offer images of groups to which some may not have knowledge or access. As such, television's use of stereotypes is important as it may serve as a crash course in what a group is like in everyday life. What becomes problematic is the application of these generalities. While monolithic phrases like "All Asian people are good at math," "All black people can dance," and "All gay people are artistic," etc., are theoretically value-free, it is personal experience and contact that places value and judgment on the stereotype. *The Cosby Show* provides a good example of something that was encoded by the producers as a positive representation of a nuclear black middle class family while some (particularly black) viewers decoded the image of The Huxtables as negative for its alleged whitewashing of black experience.

Additionally, this study does not aim to render judgment on whether a stereotype can be read as positive or negative because it is my contention that those terms are highly subjective, and what might be viewed as positive to some may be negative to others. Another potent example is Will from *Will & Grace*. There are/were viewers who believe(d) Will is/was a positive televisual representation of gay men because he is well-educated, handsome, well-adjusted and a homebody who does not rely on bars and nightclubs for his entertainment and socialization. In other words, those who hold this image of Will believe he has successfully assimilated into mainstream society. However, there are viewers who believe Will is a negative televisual representation of gay men because he is rendered sexless and unsuccessful in love (with the exception of the later seasons of the show). Put another way, Will is domesticated and unthreatening and perhaps "less gay" because of his perceived sexlessness. As Richard Dyer (2006) points out, "it is often assumed that the aim of character construction should be the creation of 'realistic individuals', but... this may have as many drawbacks as its apparent opposite, 'unreal' stereotypes." (p. 353) In other words, with televisual constructions, each viewer will decode a characterization differently. For every gay man who sees himself in Will, there is likely an equal number who see themselves in his friend Jack.

There is a school of thought that holds that, in order for gay men and women to be accepted into the mainstream, they must assimilate—erasing those traits that are deemed "too gay." Put another way, Will is a nonthreatening gay man in that he does not force heterosexual viewers to think about the sexual part of being homosexual. The contrarian view is that "assimilation into the mainstream...require[s] both a near total erasure of difference and a kind of identitarian eugenics to weed out traits, occupations, or behaviors that have been deemed too embarrassing for public view" (Harris, 2006, p. 30). Those who hold this view believe that a character like Jack on *Will & Grace* is more "gay positive" because he freely discusses his sexual trysts and can be considered "more obviously gay" than Will in that he is more flamboyant, which underscores the idea that there is no consensus on the definition of a positive or negative stereotype, particularly as it relates to the presentation of gay men on television.

Bringing blackness and gayness into the discussion of televisual stereotypes of gay men, Jasmine Cobb and Robin Means Coleman (2007) believe that:

> ...the depiction of cautiously gay characters like Carter Heywood on ABC's Spin City offers viewers a quietly conservative black man whose subdued sexuality does not thwart his professionalism in a New York City mayor's office. Since Carter's sexuality is couched in

his meticulousness, … sober disposition, and …extreme reliability, ultimately his gay identity appears less visible, less problematic and more palatable for prime time television.

Clearly, Cobb and Coleman see many of the depictions of gay black men on television as assimilationist but it is worth noting that, while there have not been as many gay black male characters on television as gay white characters, there is still a range of characters being offered—from Antoine Merriweather and Blaine Edwards on *In Living Color* who exhibit "hypersexual, highly sissified mannerisms, and high couture style" (Cobb et al., 2007) to Keith Charles on *Six Feet Under* who could be called assimilationist in that he is incorporated into a "hegemonic white world void of any hint of African American traditions, social struggle, racial conflicts, and cultural difference" (Gray, 1995a, p. 85). But as Dyer states: "…thinking about images of gayness needs to go beyond simply dismissing stereotypes as wrong or distorted" (2006, p. 353).

This study seeks to move beyond deciding what is positive or negative and instead look at the "traditional" masculinity/femininity binary along which the men of *Noah's Arc* are constructed to determine whether a hegemonic, heterosexist structure exists within the show, although it is created by a gay black man about gay black men.

Constructing Televisual Gayness

Heteronormativity is often a driving force in televisual portrayals of gay men on television, particularly those on network television. Unless told otherwise, we assume a character is heterosexual. Of course, many male characters exhibit "undeniable" traits that mark them as homosexual including being feminine and flamboyant in the vein of Jack McFarland on *Will & Grace*. While there is certainly truth to all stereotypes, the problematic associated with this construction lies in the unchecked notion that all gay men are over(t)ly feminine. Coupled with the relative lack of same-sex desire, televisual gay men are often constructed as sexless and devoid of other same-sex peers to foster a sense of community. What is at work, televisually speaking, is the construction of gay men as less than men—occupying a purgatory between the masculine and the feminine. Televisual gay men seem to be constructed in a manner that places a preference on gayness rather than maleness and robs them of their masculinity, rendering them homosexually sexless and heteronormatively harmless.

The problem is exacerbated when blackness is overlaid with televisual gayness, placing the men of *Noah's Arc* (and black gayness) squarely between blackness and gayness. As Herman Gray (1995b) says, the popular culture construction of black masculinity is exemplified by "drugs, sexism, pleasure, excess, nihilism, defiance, pride and the cool pose of disengagement" and is all part of the "style, personality, vision and practice of an assertive heterosexual black masculinity." (p. 401) Since the men of *Noah's Arc* do not conform to Gray's assertion about the construction of black masculinity and since gayness is televisually constructed as whiteness, black gay maleness is not coded at all.

Methodology

To answer whether or not the characters on *Noah's Arc* exhibit what can be termed stereotypical behavior, this paper draws on a 1987 study by sociologists Mary Kite and Kay Deaux, which examined the degree to which heterosexuals ascribe opposite gender attributes to homosexuals. Put another way, are gay men more like heterosexual women than they are like heterosexual men? The current study draws from Kite and Deaux's by examining whether or not the attributes that heterosexuals ascribe to gay men could be observed in a situation comedy created by a gay black man about gay black men.

The nine, approximately 30-minute episodes that constitute the first season of *Noah's Arc* were analyzed for content and coded. The coding focused on some of the attributes most associated with male homosexuals and male heterosexuals, as found in Kite and Deaux's study on gender belief systems (1987). These attributes for male homosexuals include: 1) [speaks in a] high-pitched voice, 2) has feminine mannerisms, 3) has feminine qualities, 4) speaks with a lisp and 5) wears feminine clothing. For male heterosexuals, the list includes: 1) athletic, 2) strong and 3) married. The attributes found in Kite and Deaux's study that will not be tested for homosexual males are: 1) positive toward males, 2) can look like any person, and 3) friendly. For heterosexual males, "positive toward females" and "normal" will not be tested. These attributes were excluded because they are largely unquantifiable and are not explained in the study.

Results and Discussion

Speaking in a High Pitched Voice

The nine episodes of *Noah's Arc* revealed that characters exhibited five instances of speaking with a high-pitched voice. The behavior was exhibited by two of the show's main characters, Noah (40 percent) and Alex (60 percent), and included instances of screeching and high-pitched laughter. Speaking with a lisp was not coded in this section, but was recognized in one character, Alex, as will be discussed below.

Having Feminine Qualities

The second stereotype observed in the nine episodes of *Noah's Arc* were characters having feminine qualities. This was observed twice and by only one character, Noah. In one instance, Noah is in a bar trying to gather his nerves to dance with a man at the bar he and his friends frequent. (The man is Wade and ultimately becomes his boyfriend). His friends try to warn him that he is about to drink alcohol (Jack Daniels and Coke) but they are too late, and Noah downs the drink in one gulp, resulting in his choking. The second instance also occurs in a bar setting, this time one frequented by Noah's boyfriend Wade, who has newly come out as gay, and his (Wade's) heterosexual friends who have gathered to play pool. While the heterosexual men order beer, Noah orders an apple martini, setting up a dichotomy between heterosexual and gay men: "real men" drink beer and "others," particularly gay men, drink mixed drinks. Here, even in a show written by a gay black man, gay black men are "othered."

It can be argued that this occurrence speaks to an anti-assimilationist agenda by the writer/producer of the show, Patrik-Ian Polk, which seeks to create a black queer identity that eschews "accepted" televisual representations of gay black men. But given the dichotomous nature of the televisual world in which we live, these representations can be read by viewers as an "othering" of gay black men vis á vis heterosexual men and masculinity.

Having Feminine Mannerisms

The third stereotype, display of feminine mannerisms, was observed five times including fanning oneself in response to something said by another character, crossing the legs at the knee and having both legs hang (in a style more often associated with women) rather than the resting the foot on the opposite knee (in a style more often associated with men). This behavior was observed 80 percent of the time in Noah's character and 20 percent of the time in Alex's character (see Figure 1 below).

Speaking with a lisp was another characteristic that was found

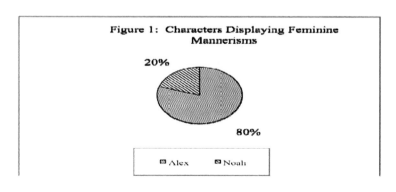

Figure 1: Characters Displaying Feminine Mannerisms

20%

80%

☐ Alex   ☒ Noah

in both Kite and Deaux's study (1987) and the current study. Only one character, Alex, spoke with a lisp. It is worth noting that some of the character's voices, most notably Noah's, could be characterized as having a feminine voice/speech pattern; however, because the behavior was being coded for lisp, rather than having a feminine vocal quality, these instances were not counted in this category.

Wearing Feminine Clothing

The last stereotype associated with gay men was the wearing of feminine clothing. That trait was observed 23 times over the course of the nine-episode period or an average of about 2.5 times each episode. The character observed wearing feminine clothing most often was Noah, who was observed wearing feminine clothing 16 times for a total

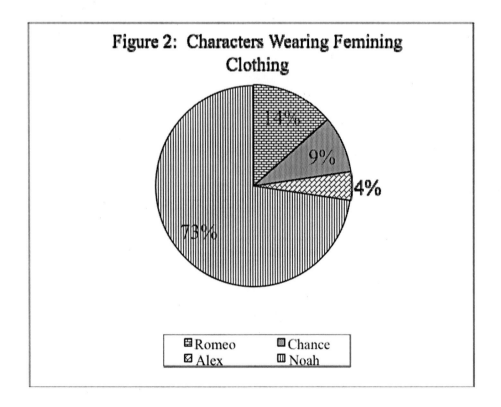

Figure 2: Characters Wearing Feminine Clothing

14%
9%
4%
73%

Romeo   Chance
Alex   Noah

of 72.73 percent of the occurrences (see Figure 2 on previous page). The clothing included Ugg boots, cropped jackets, flowers on clothing (in the style of Sarah Jessica Parker's character Carrie Bradshaw on *Sex in the City*), kimono, ponchos and a purse. Romeo, a minor guest character who appeared in two episodes, was observed wearing feminine clothing three times (13.64 percent), followed by Chance wearing feminine clothing twice (9.09 percent) and lastly Alex, who was observed once (4.55 percent). When coding this section, instances of characters in drag were not included because those were instances in which the goal was to wear a costume that emulated a woman's style of dress rather than wearing feminine clothing in everyday life.

Athleticism

When examining the stereotypes that Kite and Deaux's respondents ascribed to heterosexual men, athleticism was observed three times by the characters Wade (twice) and Ricky (once). The first episode in the series constructs Wade as a heterosexual man and, as such, he displays some athletic prowess including playing basketball in one episode and rollerblading in another. Although the viewer later finds out that Wade is gay, Noah (and the episode synopsis) in the pilot episode "My One Temptation" uses the phrase "obviously straight" to describe him. In the same episode, it is important to note that the viewer first meets the character Wade rollerblading and flirting with (and getting the phone number of) a woman. Only Ricky is shown displaying some rollerblading prowess.

This is juxtaposed against the other three characters, Noah, Alex and Chance, who are unable to rollerblade in the first episode of the show. It is also worth nothing that Ricky is the most sexually uninhibited character in the episode, regularly engaging in sexual relationships with a variety of sexual partners. The character Ricky, through his sexual conquests (which never lead to any kind of lasting relationship), is set up as being on the more masculine end of the gay spectrum than the other characters with whom he is friendly. But it is important to note that, while it was not a stereotype ascribed to gay men in the Kite and Deaux study, Ricky's promiscuity conforms to heteronormative notions of oversexed and lascivious gay men. So, while sexual conquest/prowess is often a demarcation of black masculinity, it is an attribute ascribed to gay men, particularly in the debate about same sex marriage.

Being Strong

Physical strength was observed in one character, Trey, who is Alex's partner. The character has a bodybuilder-type body and is called on once by his partner Alex to lift something that he (Alex) cannot because he is presumably the weaker of the two. Alex says, "Look at my man! He's so big and strong," setting up the dichotomy between physical strength (masculinity) and weakness (femininity). Additionally, in the scenes wherein the two of them have sex, Alex assumes the more sexually passive (receiver) role, while Trey assumes the more sexually active (inserter) role.

Getting Married

Talk of getting married/husbands is observed six times with the word "husband" being observed three times (or 50 percent of the occurrences). These occurrences were divided evenly between Alex and Chance when referring to their partners. Alex also uses the word "husband" to refer to Wade once he and Noah enter into a relationship. The use of the word "husband" is important given the heteronormative construction of marriage and the federal legal exclusion of gay men and lesbians from the institution. Proposition 8 was not yet a consideration in California, where the characters reside.

The use of the word "husband" is also interesting particularly given Alex's construction as a feminine character and the way in which his ongoing relationship is constructed along a masculine/feminine binary.

Analysis

What becomes clear is that Noah and Alex are the two major characters who are coded as feminine by the producer and writers of *Noah's Arc*. While Chance appears in categories where feminine attributes could be ascribed to him, it is Noah and Alex who appear in the most categories. This becomes problematic particularly because these two men are the ones who are observed most frequently within the context of a romantic relationship with men who most frequently demonstrate masculine attributes as constructed by the Kite and Deaux study. For example, Noah appears in all of the feminine categories except one, while Ricky, for the characteristics observed in the current study, was observed in none. Additionally, Alex appears in all of the feminine categories.

In the relatively steady relationships on the show, the dichotomous nature in which the characters are portrayed becomes clearer. All of the relationships are constructed from a heteronormative perspective, which is problematic because it reinforces heterosexist notions of homosexual relationships (i.e., gay relationships are comprised of a traditionally "male" and a "female" figure). Additionally, while certainly some relationships are constructed this way in everyday life, this is the only available construction of same-sex relationships on *Noah's Arc* and is often the way in which televised homosexual relationships are constructed (there are a few relationships not constructed in this manner like David and Keith on *Six Feet Under* and Will and Vince on *Will & Grace*). In Noah and Wade's relationship, Noah, who appears in most of the feminine categories, is paired with Wade, who appears in none of the feminine categories and is portrayed, based on this study, as athletic. In Alex and Trey's relationship, Alex appears in all of the feminine categories while Trey is portrayed as a strong, masculine character, not exhibiting any characteristics termed feminine. Romeo and Raphael's relationship (two minor characters on the show) is set up in this manner as well. Romeo is observed in feminine clothing three times on the show, including carrying a purse in one instance, while Raphael appears in none of the categories that were tested in the current study.

The data show that the characters on *Noah's Arc* utilize the stereotypes of gay men more often than those attributed to heterosexual men, based on the findings of Kite and Deaux's study. Taken in full, there were nine instances of stereotypically heterosexual male behaviors (or an average of one per episode) while there were 36 instances of stereotypically homosexual male behaviors (or an average of four instances per episode), leading to the conclusion that *Noah's Arc* does, in fact, rely on gay stereotypes (at least as set forth by the Kite and Deaux study) for the development of its characters. This is particularly important because it demonstrates that, even as *Noah's Arc* is a show created by a gay black man about gay black men, it reinforces the notion that gay and masculine are discordant.

Tele-visually, gay black men tend to be constructed as less manly dating back to *In Living Color* and continuing through to *Noah's Arc*. The exception to this rule typically occurs when gay black men are in cross-racial relationships (like on *GR∑∑K* and *Six Feet Under*) where black gay men's masculinity is emphasized in juxtaposition to their white partners.

It is important to note that, while this study found that the characters on *Noah's Arc* exhibit gay stereotypical behavior four times as often as heterosexual stereotypes, this study makes no attempt to classify these behaviors as positive or negative. Although the main characters are constructed as feminine, it still shows a range of representations of gay black men—a species rarely seen on television. In other words, as in life, there are gay black men like Noah and Alex who may exhibit behaviors that would cause many to suspect their homosexuality, thus fulfilling the promise of a stereotype. However, there are also gay black men like Trey who defy the "stereotypes" of gay men as held by heterosexuals (and even some homosexuals).

But based on this study's findings, the show's construction of gay black men relies heavily on the construction of the men of *Noah's*

Arc as feminine. As such, the viewer could receive the message that gayness is equated with femininity (no matter the message intended) because the task of representing masculine gay characters primarily falls on minor characters. Importantly, the male characters who are present on the show, like Trey and Wade, tend to serve the purpose of reinforcing heteronormative and heterosexist notions about gay relationships (namely, that there is a "man" and a "woman" in the relationship, even when the two people involved are of the same gender). *Noah's Arc* certainly adds to the visibility of gay black men on television, but could have benefitted from a more calibrated and nuanced representation by constructing some of the main characters (perhaps two of the four main characters) as more masculine and others as less masculine, thereby offering a wider spectrum of what it means to be a gay black man (on television). *Noah's Arc* would/could be as easily criticized had the show chosen to represent all gay black men as "straight" as Will Truman or had they used a hyper-masculine model to create the characters.

There is space to celebrate all stereotypes because they are all grounded in a kernel of truth. There are gay black men out there for whom Noah is reminiscent of themselves or someone they know. Still, there are others who are using television generally, and *Noah's Arc* specifically, as a looking glass. This group may be turned away from *Noah's Arc* because of the over(t)ly feminine qualities that the men of *Noah's Arc* present and find the representation is discordant with their self image or that of their peer group.

Under the heteronormative construction of masculinity (which does not carve out a space for gay masculinity) and the construction of gayness (which is white and male), it becomes important for the men of *Noah's Arc* (and televised gay men, generally) to assert their masculinity and maleness. Gay men are often culturally associated with the feminine, and femininity is culturally associated with weakness, thus coding gay men as weak.

While *Noah's Arc* fails to construct black gayness differently than other popular culture representations that rob gay black men of their masculinity (unless in interracial relationships like Keith Charles on *Six Feet Under*), it creates representation of gay black men in a televised space that largely constructs gayness as whiteness as evidenced by the relatively small number of gay black male characters on television. The call is not for a singular "approved" representation of gay black men that rely on the stereotype of gay black men as feminine (like Antoine Meriwether and Blaine Edwards), but more nuanced televise representation (in a single show) that allow for feminine characters with masculine characters and not just for the purpose of making homosexual relationships conform to heteronormative idea(l)s about gay relationships.

References

Associated Press. (2005, April 13). New networks seek gay, lesbian audiences. Retrieved from http://www.usatoday.com/life/television/news/2005-04-13-gay-networks_x.htm

Berry, G.L. (1980). Television and Afro-Americans: Past legacy and present portrayals. In Withey, S. B. and Abeles, R. P. (Eds.) *Television and social behavior.* Hillsdale, NJ: Lawrence Erlbaum Associates.

Clark, C. C. (1969). Television and social controls: Some observations on the portrayals of ethnic minorities. *Television Quarterly 2*, 18-22.

Cobb, J. & Means-Coleman, R. (2007). Two snaps and a twist: Controlling images of black male homosexuality on television. Paper presented at the annual meeting of the International Communication Association, San Francisco, CA, May 23, 2007.

Dyer, R. (2006). Stereotyping. In Durham, M. & and Kellner, D. M., *Media and cultural studies: Key works.* Malden, MA: Blackwell Publishing.

Fisher, D. A., Hill, D.L., Grube J. W. & Gruber, E. L. (2007). Gay, lesbian and bisexual content on television: A quantitative analysis across two seasons. *Journal of Homosexuality 52*, 167-188.

Fouts, G. & Inch, R. (2005). Homosexuality in TV situation comedies: Characters and verbal comments. *Journal of Homosexuality 49*, 35-45.

Gray, H. (1995a). *Watching race: Television and the struggle for blackness*. Minneapolis: University of Minnesota Press.

Gray, H. (1995b). Black masculinity and visual culture. *Callaloo 18*, 401-405.

Harris, W.C. (2006). Queer eye on the prize: The stereotypical sodomites of summer. In Keller, J. R. & Stratyner, L., *The new queer aesthetic on television*. Jefferson, NC: McFarland Press.

Lippman, W. (1922). *Public opinion*. New York: Harcourt.

Odenwald, D. (2004). *Noah's Arc: Reel affirmations*. Retrieved from http://www.metroweekly.com/feature/reel_affirmations_2004/?id=13.

Payne, M. A. (1994). "The 'ideal' black family?: A Carribean view of *The Cosby Show*." *Journal of Black Studies 25*, 231-249.

Raley, A. B. & Lucas, J.L. (2006). Stereotypes or success? Prime-time television's portrayals of gay male, lesbian, and bisexual characters. *Journal of Homosexuality 51*, 19-38.

Ward, M. L. (2004). Wading through the stereotypes: Positive and negative associations between media use and black adolescents' conceptions of self. *Developmental Psychology 40*, 284-294.

Biography

Alfred L. Martin, Jr., is a Ph.D. student at The University of Texas at Austin studying Media Studies with an emphasis on the televise construction of sexuality, race and gender. He has presented work at conferences including the American Sociological Association and the Association of Black Sociologists, has written for *Pop Matters*, and has been interviewed as an expert on media-related topics for bankrate.com, forbes.com, mint.com and Edge Publications. Martin can be reached via email at al.martin@mail.utexas.edu.

"Quittin' Time!" Exploring Black Masculinities in the Film *Gone With The Wind*

Jay Poole, Ph.D.

University of North Carolina, Greensboro

Abstract

The 1939 film, Gone With The Wind, *noted as a cinematic masterpiece, offers opportunities to explore constructions of black masculinities. Focused on two primary black male characters, Big Sam (Everett Brown) and Pork (Oscar Polk), this article considers stereotypic constructions of the "black rapist" and "Uncle Tom." Additionally, queer reading practices are utilized to examine how black masculine stereotypes may be (re)imagined. The impact of traditional gender roles is discussed and possibilities for how they can be read are taken up through an apparent moral act that turns a would-be villain into a hero.*

Introduction

The 1939 film *Gone With The Wind* has been noted as one of the best films of all time. Many hail its technical qualities as well as its aesthetics as a cinematic masterpiece with its sweeping vistas and portrayal of the Old South as it crumbled during the United States Civil War. Produced by David O. Selznick, the film was based on the novel by Margaret Mitchell, who had heard the stories of the Civil War from her Georgia-based family as she grew up in the 1920s. The novel and film are filled with multidimensional characters including those who had been enslaved by white plantation owners in the pre-Civil War South. Notably, representations of masculinity are peppered throughout the characters in *Gone With The Wind* including those who are African American.

At the surface, the enslaved characters the viewer comes to know as the film progresses may be read as stereotypic—I will keep the doting mammy, the soft-spoken butler, the silly house girl, and the strapping field hand; yet, if one begins to read below the surface, interesting commentaries emerge. In particular, dimensions of black masculinities may be examined through engagement with the characters Big Sam (Everett Brown), the foreman of the O'Hara plantation, and Pork (Oscar Polk), who is the butler for the O'Hara household. Through these two characters, viewers are exposed to traditional images of black masculinity and, perhaps less obviously, different images of black masculinities. The characters convey narratives about power, and its location in traditional notions of black maleness, contextualized within a complex structure of gender norms, are explored. *Gone With The Wind* reflects the American South just prior to and after the Civil War asserting that the economic devastation of the South shifted identities for whites and blacks. The residue of what it meant/means to be a black male continues to trickle through social and cultural beliefs and practices despite the shift in identities.

Grounded in hierarchy and steeped in patriarchy, masculinities, regardless of ethnic or racial influences, seem to maintain identities that stem from cultural morays reified through the use of humans by other humans for the exploitation of resources and the production of goods that results in economic gain for those who are privileged, e.g., the white plantation/business owner. Here, two principal African American male characters in *Gone With The Wind* are used to consider how power operates within so-called traditional constructions of black masculinity and within and among broader constructions of masculinities. Additionally, the promise of re-imagining black masculinities is explored.

Tradition and Masculinities

Notions of masculinity are varied and have been the subject of critique for quite some time, but especially since the advent of the so-called women's movement (Messner, 1997). Perhaps it is through lenses of feminism that masculinities are most carefully examined with particular attention to how patriarchy operates through and within traditionally defined masculine ideals. Of course, feminism and feminist theorizing has been dominated by white women of privilege with the voices of marginalized women rising only in the so-called third wave of feminism (Tarrant, 2006). It is within the third wave and perhaps a fourth that the experiences of individuals in the margins begins to become noted and such discourse includes the examination of men in the margins. Questions about how and why masculinities are constructed in particular ways can be and are being asked. Images of masculinity take shape and a core image is that of the traditionally masculine.

Peter Murphy (2001) discusses the image of man, constructed traditionally, as machine and suggests that, "The most powerful cultural metaphor for masculinity is the machine, a cold, disembodied efficacious piece of equipment . . ." (p. 33). Indeed, manliness, defined within traditional views, seems to be very mechanical and men with machine-like bodies are deemed best to produce. The penis becomes the site of production (quite literally) and, as Murphy indicates, the male experience, conceptually, is centered on erections and ejaculation. In fact, the penis and testicles are often the location of power, ridicule, and shame depending on how one's genitals are perceived by self and/or others. Size matters in all respects (legs, arms, chest, and genitals) and certainly this notion of largeness has permeated the stereotyped image of the black male.

Richardson (2007) asserts that regional influences, especially from the South, have played a major role in the construction of particular black masculinities, and *Gone With The Wind* exhibits two prominent and opposing stereotypes that seem to be dominant through Big Sam and Pork; the large strapping "black buck" in Big Sam's character, with physical attributes that are often presumed to represent the black rapist, and the docile and apparently subservient "Uncle Tom" stereotype represented in Pork's character. Indeed, the film turns the viewer on edge when Big Sam turns out to be a savior for the heroine, Scarlett O'Hara (Vivian Leigh). Apparently, David O. Selznick was very attentive to the representation of slavery in the film and was adamant about minimizing the degradation of the black characters (Crips, 1983; Selznick, 1988). Selznick's awareness of the cultural climate in America and internationally during the late Depression years, as well as the evolving climate of racial tension with the enforcement of the Jim Crow laws in the South and the persecution of Jews in Germany, seemed to play a role in creating black characters that were human, particularly when historical accuracy called for blacks to be conceived as less than human; the property of wealthy whites.

Interestingly, the portrayal of slavery in *Gone With The Wind* is softened and often sympathetic with the viewer knowing only a few enslaved characters whose loyalty to their owners is more familial rather than subservient. Certainly, the despicable practice of buying and selling human beings for the purpose of economic growth is not prominent in *Gone With The Wind* as we see slaves there as extensions of the white owner families, blurring the lines between master/servant. A particular example of this may be found in the dynamics between Scarlett and her "Mammy" (Hattie McDaniel), seeming to be more like mother/daughter than a wealthy white woman of privilege and an enslaved woman of African descent who is powerful in her own right.

Pork: Passive and Dependent?

Rowan (1993) points out that Pork, the stereotypic Uncle Tom character, seems to be represented as unified with Scarlett in the quest to save Tara, the family plantation despite his being enslaved for what we may presume has been most of his life. Joining with Scarlett, his white owner, may be read as representing a particular masculine role for black males; support those in power and work with them in order to perpetuate your own well-being, even if this means foregoing personal aspirations. Another reading may highlight Pork's humanness in his attempt to help Scarlett negotiate the dilemma and genuine concern about what has been his home. This image of the subservient black male has been codified as being an "Uncle Tom," taken from the main character of the famous Harriet Beecher Stowe 1851 novel, *Uncle Tom's Cabin* (Morgan, 2007). Actually, Uncle Tom in Stowe's novel is quite convicted about seeking his freedom and he sacrifices himself for the freedom of others, yet, he is often conceived through stereotype as passive. This misreading of the Uncle Tom character has perpetuated the notion that passive black males may be questionable with regard to their masculinities.

Noting the juxtaposition of Tom's perceived passivity as "feminine" and the "masculine" stance of the three women whose bravery and perseverance allow an escape from slavery, Williams (2002) asserts that Stowe, knowingly or not, was commenting on the reversal of traditional gender roles by emasculating Tom and empowering the women with what are conceptualized as traditionally masculine characteristics: individualism, self-sufficiency, bravery, rational thinking, and perseverance. In *Gone With The Wind*, Pork is portrayed as passive and becomes emotionally expressive when he is discussing the fate of Tara with Scarlett.

Similar to Williams's (2002) reading of the dynamics in *Uncle Tom's Cabin*, Scarlett, the woman, has to take control and make decisions in order to keep the family afloat, and it is her presumed bravery, labor in the fields, and perseverance that restores Tara to its grandeur. Pork is supportive and concerned and, ultimately, because of his commitment to Scarlett, is able to remain as her butler in the mansion she eventually acquires. He memorably says in the scene where he, Mammy, and Prissy (Butterfly McQueen) walk through the gate and see the opulent mansion before them, "Great Je-ho-sa-phat!" (*Gone With The Wind*, 1939). The line indicates his astonishment and presumed personal pleasure at being able to live in such a fine home. Notably, we are to assume that no black person could afford such finery and further, Pork, Mammy, and Prissy, because of their undying allegiance to their former white owner, are elated to be "rich" as evidenced by Prissy's line, "Darkies, we sure is rich now!" (*Gone With The Wind*, 1939). The image of Pork as subservient, dependant, and passive represents what may be perceived as a feminized version of black masculinity. The stereotyped "Uncle Tom" seems to capture a black masculine identity that locates itself in what may be perceived as feminine spaces, if we define the feminine in traditional ways – passive, emotional, and dependent. Perhaps Pork may be read simply as humane and genuinely concerned about others despite having been owned by them. In any case, working in the binary, one presumes that the opposite of the Uncle Tom is mythologically powerful, independent, and perhaps dangerous black male who engages in hard labor, exhibits bravery, and lusts after white women; not to mention that he is well endowed.

Big Sam: Villain or Hero?

Big Sam, early in *Gone With The Wind*, asserts his position as the foreman of Tara and, as his name indicates, embodies the strong field hand whose labor is the foundation of all the wealth enjoyed in the Old South. The image is powerful as one views the film: A row of presumably black men is plowing a field with horses and one of them yells, "Quittin' time!" In response to this, Big Sam corrects the insubordination and says, "Who says it quittin' time? I's the foreman and I's the one who says it's quittin' time at Tara!" Without missing a beat, he turns and yells to his subordinates, "Quittin' time!" With that, the scene cross-fades into a pastoral scenario of the slaves leaving the fields compete with a melodic score. As one digest this small but important scene, it seems clear that, within the ranks of slavery, the hierarchy denoted in the binary of master/servant is prevalent and, further, it is the strongest of men that rise to power in the struggle to discover just who is the boss. This reflection of hierarchical power is dominant in white culture with white men of wealth and privilege enjoying high social standing. It seems that *Gone With The Wind* illustrates how white constructions of power operating in hierarchy permeated the ranks of enslaved people of African descent as illustrated by Big Sam's assertion that he has earned the privilege of being in charge. Interestingly, the stereotype of black masculinity that is represented through Big Sam also bodes a darker aspect with regard to sexuality.

Lemelle (2010) and Matthews (2009) identify the perpetuation of the myth of the sexually charged black male as rapist to instill fear among southern whites and justify lynching, particularly in the South during reconstruction. The black rapist myth imagines the freed male slave as determined to seek revenge on whites for being held captive. Fueled by anger and sexual desire, the black rapist ravages white women asserting his power through sexual means.

The black rapist functions in the binary as the antithesis of the stereotypic "Uncle Tom" and encapsulates all that is to be feared with regard to black men. Big Sam is poised via stereotypic construction to fit the villainous black rapist stereotype in *Gone With The Wind*; yet, the viewer is challenged when he becomes a hero. The viewer is not led to understand that Big Sam is particularly close to Scarlett. Indeed, their relationship is not portrayed as particularly close as we only see them together in two scenes. Scarlett recognizes Big Sam in the streets of Atlanta when the city is in chaos just before Sherman takes control of it. Big Sam updates Scarlett about what has happened at Tara and reports that he is going to help the southern troops in their effort to fend off Sherman. Both Scarlett and Big Sam go on their ways. Later in the film, Scarlett is driving her buggy through a less than desirable location when men who presumably want to rob and rape her stage an attack. It happens that Big Sam, who has presumably become a ne'er-do-well, is in residence in the "shanty town" and, hearing her cries, recognizes that it is his former owner and comes to her rescue. What is notable about the scene is that the attackers are a white man, presumably of lower class, and a black man, presumably a former slave who fits that black rapist mythical image. Indeed, the viewer is challenged by the fact that the white man, who appears to be on the verge of raping Scarlett, is attacked and beaten by Big Sam in his attempt to rescue her. The black man, whom he overcomes and throws into the river, then attacks Big Sam. Ultimately, Scarlett is rescued by Big Sam, who is rewarded by her husband with cash and sent off to Tara where he can presumably take up his position as foreman again. On the surface, the scene may be read as an example of dedication and commitment on the part of Big Sam despite his being enslaved. The viewer may interpret that he has made a mistake by trying to be "free" and that he is better off going back to Tara and his former owners. However, if one deconstructs that scene, images of masculinity and power abound.

The fact that Scarlett was riding in her buggy alone denotes a practice unbecoming to women in that era. She carries a pistol and owns a business. She dominates her husband by making decisions on his behalf. She has become ruthless in her pursuit of wealth. Scarlett, at this point in the film, behaves more like a man than a woman, according to Rhett Butler, her long-time suitor. Yet, in this scene, she is vulnerable to the likes of the stereotypic black rapist.

Interestingly, choices about who attacks her seem to echo Selznick's attention to the racial tensions that were building in the late 1930s in America as he casts that primary attacker as a white man. Of course, his accomplice is an African American male who we presume will have his way with Scarlett. Big Sam, who fits the physical image of the stereotypic black rapist, becomes a hero by overcoming not only another black male, but a white man as well. The person, historically contextualized as less than human, who would be Scarlett's rapist according to the mythical stereotype, becomes her savior.

Big Sam is played as a person of morals despite who he is supposed to be, and the message of the scene becomes one of acting on morals rather than carnal desire. The fact that Big Sam is capable of being a moral person seems to disrupt the immoral black rapist stereotype and calls into question its existence in the mythology of black masculinities. Of course, the notion that Big Sam is better off going back to the plantation plays into the idea that freed slaves simply did not know how privileged they were to be take care of by their owners, perpetuating the myth that blacks are dependant on whites for their livelihoods. Big Sam had "quit" his life at Tara only to discover that the promises of the carpetbaggers from the north were empty. This image of the moral black man as dependent denotes yet another nuance in the construction of black masculinities as expectations about independence and self-sufficiency are challenged.

The idea that black males are inferior stems from the complex web of social and cultural beliefs and practices that operate in spaces dominated by white people (Coleman, 2008; Lemelle, 2010; Richardson, 2007). Asserting that black males often internalize racism, Coleman (2008) points out that black masculinities may be characterized by reactionary and oppositional positions due to the notion that black skin is inferior as perpetuated in a social structure dominated by white hegemony. Thus, despite his heroism, Big Sam remains inferior to his former white owners. The message about black masculinities seems to be with both Pork and Big Sam that, as a black man, one should recognize the importance of this allying with white people of status, as this may be the only way one can enjoy a "good" life.

Being Empowered

Richardson (2005) points out that Southern black males have been particularly typed as inferior even to black males from other regions; thus, the struggle for social position and citizenship is even more challenging for black males of Southern origin. Perhaps, as Friend and Glover (2004) note, the experience of slavery involved a process of emasculation for those males who were dominated by their owners, creating a cultural residue that fueled a quest for reclaiming so-called masculinity through violence. Kimmell (2000) asserts that violence is the dominant means of demonstrating manhood sociologically, and traditional constructions of masculinity emphasize violence as an expression of power. To become empowered, one must act violently, asserting authority and claiming dominance. If we consider the slave owner's power over those who were enslaved, we can imagine how one learned to be a man, particularly in the American South. Real men were powerful through ownership and owning things meant exploiting resources, including human resources. In order to quell any uprising or rebellion, harsh punishment to the point of death was utilized to control those who were insubordinate. In *Gone With The Wind*, the former white slave owners, after they have sent Big Sam off to Tara, go after those who attacked Scarlett in order to (re)assert power over those who were previously owned.

This banter of power, centered on who holds the locus of control, plays out repeatedly as males and, in many cases, females attempt to negotiate masculinity. As Wendt (2007) notes, the struggle for power was particularly complex as non-violent approaches were adopted during the Civil Rights era in the United States. Tension between the notion that being armed for self-defense and the notion that one could peacefully protest injustice was high and the sense of being emasculated was present as people were asked to act passively. Cultural reflections of the tension between the Uncle Tom and the black rapist stereotypes can be seen today as one considers passive versus militant activism with regard to masculinities.

As Richardson (2007) asserts, the "gangsta" image seems to repackage traditional militant activism as it (re)claims power. *Gone With The Wind* shows us a subtext of the active/passive binary as Pork and Big Sam, owned by the same family, express their loyalties differently; Big Sam acts with defensive aggression and violence while Pork passively discusses the future of Tara with Scarlett, empowering her to act. It is this ongoing tension within and among the active/passive that becomes intriguing as one considers black masculinities and how they may be imagined beyond the binary. Does empowerment lie in acts that are selfless and considerate? Is collaboration and cooperation potential characteristics that have empowering possibilities in (re)imagined masculinities? While *Gone*

With The Wind does not answer these questions, it may spark us to think about them and about the possibilities of masculinities beyond the traditional.

Conclusions

Images of black masculinity in the United States are varied and evolving; yet, there seem to be some foundational aspects of the black man that are grounded in traditional constructions of masculine. Of course, the construction of what has come to be framed as traditional began within cultural spaces dominated by white males who possessed material wealth including owning other human beings. Power, seems to be at the center of what it means to be masculine, with power being contextualized in binaural constructions of strong v. weak and active v. passive. Those with strength, particularly physical and emotional strength, are deemed to be more masculine, and those who are physically and emotionally vulnerable are often labeled as feminine. Depending on others is not a traditional characteristic of manliness; rather, a man must be independent and able to function autonomously. To be a man in the traditional sense involves physical and emotional strength, independence, upward mobility, and possession of wealth. As this construction of masculine evolved in American culture, it permeated notions of gender regardless of other identity labels including racially based identities. The black man, though a white man may have owned him, was subjected to meanings of masculinity that ultimately reflected dominant cultural paradigms.

Gone With The Wind, constructed during and reflective of a time in America when racial tensions were rising and the promise of Civil Rights was in the air, offers the viewer images of black masculinities that are traditional in the sense that they express passive and active approaches; yet, they disrupt expectations as villain becomes hero. Perhaps a small and probably unintended subtext may be read if one imagines how cooperative relationships grounded in respect and concern for others may benefit all. Notably, Big Sam and Pork act with care and concern toward Scarlett and, through this action, they ensure their dignity and humanity. The image of marginalized men acting with care and concern is promising as one considers that, in 1939, race relations were inflamed domestically and internationally. As America moved toward its global position of power, what it meant/means to be a man began to evolve, though the core of man as machine seemed to stand firm.

Perhaps, through careful reflection and critical examination, masculinities can be re-visioned and re-constructed to reflect spaces beyond the active/passive and strong/weak binaries, pushing past patriarchal boundaries and into spaces that reconstruct what it might mean to be a man. Johnson II (2010) asks us to consider how patriarchy perpetuates sexism, particularly in black cultural spaces and how we might disrupt the influence of sexism as we imagine masculinities that are respectful, cooperative, and collective. Perhaps, as Big Sam said, it is "quittin' time" as we begin to slough off some of the residue of patriarchal structures for more promising ways to be men. Indeed, the promise of how masculinities can be imagined lies in the fact that they already have been.

References

Crips, T. (1983). Winds of change: *Gone with the wind* and racism as a national issue. Pyron, D. (Ed.). *Recasting Gone With The Wind in American Culture* (pp. 137-152). Miami: University Press of Florida.

Coleman, K. (2008). Black male politicization: Same script, different cast. *CLA Journal51*(4), 394.

Friend, C. & Glover, L. (2004). Rethinking southern masculinity: An introduction. Friend, C. & Glover, L. (Eds.). *Southern Manhood: Perspectives on Masculinity in the Old South* (pp. vii-xvii). Athens, GA: University of Georgia Press.

Johnson II, B. (2010). Toward and anti-sexist black American male identity. *Psychology of Men and Masculinity11*(3), 182-194.

Lemelle, A. (2010). *Black masculinity and sexual politics*. New York: Routledge.

Kimmel, M. (2000). *The Gendered Society*. New York: The Oxford University Press.

Matthews, D. (2009). The southern rite of human sacrifice: Lynching in the American south. *Mississippi Quarterly62*(1), 27-70.

Messner, M. (1997). *Politics of Masculinities: Men in Movements.* Thousand Oaks, CA: Sage.

Morgan, J. (2007). *Uncle Tom's Cabin as Visual Culture.* Columbia, MO: University of Missouri Press.

Richardson, R. (2007). *Black Masculinity and the U.S. South: From Uncle Tom to Gangsta.* Athens, GA: University of Georgia Press.

Richardson, R. (2005). Charles Fuller's southern specter and the geography of black masculinity. *American Literature77*(1), 7-32.

Rowan, C. (1993). Gone with the wind, and good riddance. *Southwest Review78*(3), 377.

Selznick, J. (Producer), Thompson, D. (Screenwriter), Hinton, D. (Director). (1988). *The Making of a Legend: Gone with the Wind* [Motion Picture]. United States: Elstree Ltd.

Selznick, D. (Producer), Howard, S. & Selznick, D. (Screenwriters), Fleming, V. (Director). (1939). *Gone with the Wind* [Motion Picture]. United States: Selznick International Pictures.

Tarrant, S. (2006). When Sex Became Gender (Perspectives on Gender). New York: Routledge.

Wendt, S. (2007). They finally found out that we are really men: Violence, non-violence and black manhood in the civil rights era. *Gender and History19* (3), 543-564.

Williams, L. (2002). *Playing the Race Card: Melodramas of Black and White from Uncle Tom to O.J.* Princeton, NJ: Princeton University Press.

Biography

Dr. Jay Poole is Assistant Professor at the University of North Carolina at Greensboro in the Department of Social Work. His career in clinical social work spans over 25 years and currently he is involved with efforts to examine diversity, equity, and inclusion. One of his research interests is identity studies with particular focus on gender and sexuality. His recent work appears in *Men Speak Out: Views on Sex Power and Gender* edited by Shira Tarrant (2008) and in *Brightlights Film Journal*.

Patriotism: A Love Story

Toby S. Jenkins, Ph.D.

George Mason University

Abstract

In this article, the author offers a critical examination of the concept of patriotism from the perspective of the college experience. Drawing on examples from popular culture and current campus events, the essay advances the belief that organizational critique and social activism should be embraced as strong examples of patriotism and commitment whether on campus, in a company, or in society at large. The development of conscious, critical thinkers and committed moral agents of change is an important goal of the higher education institution.

I recently rented the film by Michael Moore (2009), *Capitalism: A Love Story*. What I most love about Moore is his consistent show of patriotism for our country. Yes, I said patriotism. He consistently does the difficult work of loving our country enough to criticize it in hopes of making it better. His films consistently touch on the need for everyday people to exercise their democratic rights. As a college professor, I am constantly working to energize this generation of young adults to engage the principles of active citizenship. And so, I could not help but to think about college students as I watched. The movie brought up memories of student protest from this time last year. Fall 2009, like many fall semesters, was filled with the energy of the start of a new school year—energy fueled by expectation. I am referring to the expectation for schools, universities, and communities to live their values. In my local area, college students at Howard University and brave youth from area high schools in Maryland were all demanding change. Having worked in the past on the other side of campus, within administration, I know how easy it is for administrators to see these students as agitators...to see protest as a problem. It is actually a solution...a wake-up call. And I'd argue that those students that dare to protest are showing more school spirit than those that simply attend every football game, wear paraphernalia, and yell their love for their school with all of their might.

In a broad sense, I am concerned that our country raises citizens that are not taught how to be critical thinkers—to question, to learn, to criticize the status quo. As a citizen, I love my country like a mother loves a child. You love your child so much that you don't want to see her do wrong and so you discipline and correct every wrong turn. We correct our children out of love. So why don't we see people that take that same approach towards their country, on their campus, or in their high school as being true patriots? Instead, we define patriotism through kind and pleasant words rather than strong and bold action. In a broad sense, we groom students to play a very docile, silent, and inactive role in school. Good students are ones that do not "talk too much" or "act out." And in recent years, Zero Tolerance policies have shown that there are potentially long and hard consequences for those students that are labeled as "troubled" (Echolm, 2010). All students with a challenging spirit and an inquisitive nature may find conflict with the social rules of conformity present in education. But, African American male students have particularly felt the weight of educational cultural norms that privilege silence, obedience, and system agreement. In his article, "The Trouble with Black Boys: The Role and Influence of Environmental and Cultural Factors on the Academic Performance of African American Males," Pedro Noguera (2002) offers the following situation as an example of how schools often push students to conform:

> A recent experience at a high school in the Bay Area
> illustrates how the interplay of these two socializing

forces—peer groups and school sorting practices—can play out for individual students. I was approached by a Black male student who needed assistance with a paper on Huckleberry Finn that he was writing for his 11th grade English class. After reading what he had written, I asked why he had not discussed the plight of Jim, the runaway slave who is one of the central characters of the novel. The student informed me that his teacher had instructed the class to focus on the plot and not to get into issues about race, since according to the teacher, that was not the main point of the story. He explained that two students in the class, both Black males, had objected to the use of the word "nigger" throughout the novel and had been told by the teacher that if they insisted on making it an issue they would have to leave the course. Both of these students opted to leave the course even though it meant they would have to take another course that did not meet the college preparatory requirements. The student I was helping explained that since he needed the class he would just "tell the teacher what he wanted to hear." (Retrieved from http://www.inmotionmagazine.com/er/pntroub1.html)

Though not the sole cause of attrition, this tendency to punish students that challenge classroom practices and to reward silence and conformity is just one of the many issues that contribute to the alarming drop out and suspension rates of young black men.

The negative relationship between black males and school systems is an issue that has been steadily growing over the last 20 years. In Garibaldi's (1992) study of the New Orleans public school system, he found that, although Black male youth only represented 43% of the educational community, they accounted for 58% of the non-promotions, 65% of the suspensions, 80% of the expulsions, and 45% of the dropouts. In 2010, The Shott Foundation published *Yes We Can, The Schott 50 State Report on Public Education and Black Males*, revealing a national graduate rate of only 47% for African American male high school students. The following is shared in the report's conclusion:

> The American educational system is systemically failing Black males. Out of the 48 states reporting, Black males are the least likely to graduate from high school in 33 states, Black and Latino males are tied for the least likely in four states, with Latino males being the least likely in an additional four states. To add insult to injury, Black male students are punished more severely for similar infractions than their White peers...They are more frequently inappropriately removed from the general education classroom due to misclassifications by the Special Education policies and practices of schools and districts. (p. 37)

Race, class, and cultural differences undoubtedly play a role in this dissonance between student and school. But these factors do not excuse bad behavior. Race and problems with the culture of schools do not erase the reality that boys are often socialized to be aggressive and external environments repeatedly fail to correct wrongdoing. Shaun Harper, Frank Harris, & Kenechukwu Mmeje (2005) brought attention to this by offering forth a theoretical model to explain the overrepresentation of college men among campus judicial offenders. In the article, they note the many factors that build bad behavior in some young men:

> According to Gilbert and Gilbert (1998) and Head (1999), parents and teachers are more forgiving of behavioral problems among boys and accept the fact that "boys will be boys." Similarly, Harper (2004)asserts that parents "communicate messages of power, toughness, and competitiveness to their young sons. No father wants his son to grow up being a 'pussy,' 'sissy,' 'punk,' or 'softy'—terms commonly associated with boys and men who fail to live up to the traditional

standards of masculinity." (p. 92) Gilbert and Gilbert also found that interests in combat, wrestling, and active play interfere with male students' abilities to concentrate in school and take their teachers (who are mostly female) seriously, which often results in classroom disruptions. Interestingly, boys are over four times more likely than girls in K-12schools to be referred to the principal's office for disciplinary infractions, suspended, or subjected to corporal punishment (Gregory,1996; Skiba, Michael, Nardo, & Peterson, 2002). Despite this, boys are still socialized to believe that they are to be rough, tough, and rugged, even if it means getting into trouble at school (Mac an Ghaill,1996)

Let's be clear, some black men whether in high school or college do "act out." And as explained in the quote above, seeds of bad behavior often take root outside of the school system. However, later in the article, the authors argue for educational institutions to transform their approach to judicial affairs even when it comes to those students that are guilty of doing wrong. A move from a stiff and procedural judicial process to a more developmental and educational process is suggested (Harper, Harris, & Mmeje, 2005). This recommendation holds strong merit. Even the truly disruptive student needs to be shown a new path. Changing the spirit and tone of school judicial policy and classroom culture could hold potential benefit for everyone involved. Though many students exhibit negative, disrespectful, and disruptive behavior in school, we know that all black boys that are suspended have not "acted out" and all young black men that find themselves permanently outside of the school system are not there because of their lack of skill, bad neighborhoods, uncaring parents, and disruptive behavior. Somewhere in the mix is a failed agreement between the student and school about what constitutes being a "good" student. I know this because I often experience it as a professional of color.

Beyond educator/student interactions, my personal experience in higher education has been one in which even co-workers who proclaim to advocate for social justice education often interpret criticism as confrontation and aggression. Colleagues often paint as a villain the co-worker who is willing to stand up and stand out—to point out the critical problems within the institution, department, or academic program. Rather than recognizing the deep commitment and love that it takes to challenge in an effort to change, colleagues often would rather not deal with the "problem colleague." And so this is an issue of defining active citizenship within all of the spaces that we occupy…our country, our companies, and our communities. We must begin to appreciate those students that whisper, speak, or scream for educational change. Isn't there broad agreement that educational reform is needed in this country? So, why does it become problematic when a single student demands this reform on their campus or in their high school classroom? Whether they are asking us to change our policies on campus hate crimes, to amend student registration procedures, or to widen the lens of our course content, students are demonstrating an outward show of activism. This is indeed how "acting out" should look.

I just recently moved to the DC area. I came from Penn State University where I served as the director of a cultural center named after Paul Robeson, another great activist in history who was persecuted for challenging the politics of the day. Though many people today applaud Paul Robeson as one of the greatest global humanitarians of his time, when he was alive, this country applied its full weight to crush him because of his outspoken work and criticism against segregation, lynching, and global oppression in Africa. Attacked as a communist because of his open sympathy for the struggles against oppression of all people, he was eventually called before the House Un-American Committee. At his hearing, Paul Robeson made history as the only person to directly challenge the committee. When asked at the hearing why he didn't just leave the United States and become an ex-patriot, he said boldly and unapologetically:

> My father was a slave and my people died to build this country, and I'm going to stay right here and have a part of it, just like you. And no fascist-minded people will drive me from it. Is that clear…you are the non-patriots, and you are the un-Americans, and you ought to be

ashamed   of   yourselves.   (Retrieved   from
http://historymatters.gmu.edu/d/6440).

And of course there is also Dr. Martin Luther King, Jr., whose
model of leadership is often praised as being inclusive, peaceful, and
accepting. Because of this, his work is relevant to this discussion.
Contrary to popular understanding, Dr. King was not the type of man to
silently accept the status quo or to engage in uncritical dialogue about
his country. In his "Letter from a Birmingham Jail," Dr. King spoke
frankly about the necessity for critical thought and social tension to
create social change. He challenged the citizens of our country to
become active agents for social justice rather than passive moderates
that sustain, through their inaction, the status quo. Making any entity
better, whether it is a school, a company, or a country is not achieved
through rhetoric that makes us feel good, but rather through action and
calls to action that inspire us to do good. Here is what King (1990) had
to say:

> But I must confess that I am not afraid of the word
> "tension." I have earnestly opposed violent tension, but
> there is a type of constructive, nonviolent tension which
> is necessary for growth...I have been gravely
> disappointed with the...moderate...who is more devoted
> to "order" than to justice; who prefers a negative peace
> which is the absence of tension to a positive peace
> which is the presence of justice. (p.291)

My hope is that we begin to view patriotism as not being
exercised through simplistic statements of blind love and praise or mild
mannered actions, but instead through a dedication to doing the hard,
challenging, and almost parental work of rearing and growing, guiding
and developing those organizations and institutions that we love. I do
believe that the ethic behind being free and open to critically challenge
one's country, college, or employer in an effort to make it better and
more accountable is something to be encouraged because it illustrates
authentic love. We did not give birth to the country we live in, the

colleges we attend, or the companies for whom we work, but we have adopted the responsibility to continue to raise each of them (to a higher level). And like any good parent, we must be actively present, engaged, and vocal through every step they take.

Bibliography

Eckholm, E. (2010) School Suspensions Lead to Legal Challenge. Extracted from the New York Times Online, http://www.nytimes.com/2010/03/19/education/19suspend.html

Garibaldi, A. (1992). Educating and motivating African American males to succeed. *Journal of Negro Education, 61*(1), 4-11.

Harper, H., Harris, F. & Mmeje, K. (2005) A Theoretical Model to Explain the Overrepresentation of College Men among Campus Judicial Offenders: Implications for campus administrators. *NASPA Journal* 42 (4), 565-588.

King, M.L. (1990). Letter from a Birmingham jail in James Washington, *A Testament of Hope: The Essential Writings and Speeches of Martin Luther King.* New York: Harper Collins.

Moore, M. (2009). *Capitalism: A Love Story.* Anchor Bay.

Nogeura, P. (2002). The Trouble with Black Boys: The role and influence of environmental and cultural factors on the academic performance of African American males.
In *Motion Magazine Online*, May 13, 2002
http://www.inmotionmagazine.com/er/pntroub1.html

Robeson, Paul. (June 12, 1956); Testimony of Paul Robeson before Committee on Un-American Activities.
Retrieved from http://historymatters.gmu.edu/d/6440

Schott Foundation for Public Education (2010). *Yes we can: The Schott 50 state report on public education and black males.* Cambridge, Massachusetts

Biography

Toby Jenkins currently serves as an Assistant Professor of Integrative Studies and Higher Education at George Mason University. Her research and professional interests focus on culture as a politic of community love and social survival; the utility of non-traditional knowledge production; and the cultural arts as a tool of social resistance. Prior to George Mason, Jenkins served as Director of the Paul Robeson Cultural Center at Penn State University and Assistant Director of the Nymburu Cultural Center at the University of Maryland, College Park.

Contact Information:

Toby S. Jenkins, Ph.D.
Assistant Professor, Integrative Studies & Higher Education
George Mason University   814-280-7948 (Mobile)
4400 University Dr.   703-993-5243 (Office)
Fairfax, VA 22030   Tjenkin8@gmu.edu

Book Review - And Then There Was Baldwin: Memory, Masculinity, and the Blues

Robert E. Randolph, Jr.
University of North Carolina, Greensboro

Review of: *The Cross of Redemption: Uncollected Writings* by James Baldwin, edited by Randall Kenan, New York: Pantheon, 2010. 304 pp.

Talking about the writer's essential tool and responsibility—to remember—Toni Morrison recalls the sheer force of nature, which never ceases to remind us that it was here first:

> You know, they straightened out the Mississippi River in places, to make room for houses and livable acreage. Occasionally, the river floods these places. 'Floods' is the word they use, but in fact it is not flooding; it is remembering. Remembering where it used to be. All water has perfect memory and is forever trying to get back to where it was. Writers are like that: remembering where we were...and the route back to our original place.

She might have been talking about such a genuine writer as Baldwin; nothing, not even all the horrors his America could conjure, could straighten him out. And so, Baldwin, this small man, does not invent but remembers—in the most immediate and desperate way imaginable—those events and incidents his country is trying to forget.

(Here, I am reminded of Othello's dying declaration: "I have done the State some service, and they know it.")

In this new collection of heretofore uncollected writings, James Baldwin "reads" America like no one ever had (and probably never will again), going about his task of disassembling the myth of American ingenuity and pluck, dismantling the ethos that undergirds American masculinity and grotesque vestiges of sexuality; and recognizing that there is yet time for America to get its act together, in essence, to live up to its various creeds of equality, fairness, and possibility.

Writing is a "Poor Boy's Game," a euphemism for boxing; but it nevertheless provides an apt description of Baldwin's skill, style, and craft. Simply, writing pits the writer against his countrymen, family, institutions, "truths," and more importantly, himself. When he critiques the country, he is critiquing himself, which is painful and tiresome work. Born in Harlem, the heart of Black America in the 1920s, Baldwin was poor, black, and gay., He saw these attributes, negatives aspects insofar as America is concerned, as his birthright. When questioned about how he became a great writer in spite of these facets, he often replied that he had "hit the jackpot," that these circumstances were so bombastic and so "terrible" he could go no farther, that they had provided him with a vantage point—"a democratic vista"—from which to critique his country.

These new pieces address the same themes of Baldwin's previous work; however, they simply provide the reader with a preponderance of "evidence of things not seen" but felt in America. Randall Kenan, the collection's capable editor, admits that this volume is but a companion to *James Baldwin: Collected Essays* (1998), which Toni Morrison edited. In tandem, each volume illuminates the other, especially this new one, which teases out nuanced structures and strictures of Baldwin oeuvre, even for a veteran/devoted Baldwin reader. Yet, for novices in particular, this collection provides a "site of memory"—as much a journalistic expression as it is the essence of intellectual rigor, all the while writing "for whosoever will." (This collection has the potential to be an excellent introduction to all of Baldwin's work as well as an introduction to the African American experience—historically, spiritually, and culturally.)

Kenan divides Baldwin's collected works neatly into the categories of essays and speeches, profiles, letters, forwards and afterwards, book reviews, and fiction. "Is A Raisin in the Sun a Lemon in the Dark?" figures prominently, especially for scholars of black masculinity.

Baldwin deftly assesses Lorraine Hansberry's play as a critique of black masculinity and the black woman's role—simultaneously necessary and nefarious—in the propagation of narrow sentimentalism:

> Each of the women, the mother, the wife, and the daughter, are, on their own levels, grappling with the problem of how to create a haven of safety for Walter, so that he can be a man, play a man's role in the world, and yet not be destroyed. It is dangerous to be an American Negro male. America has never wanted its Negroes to be men, and does not, generally, treat them as men. It treats them as mascots, pets, or things. Every Negro woman knows what her man faces when he goes out to work, and what poison he will probably bring back.

The question/issue of masculinity is replete throughout Baldwin's writings and this volume is no different; in "As Much Truth As One Can Bear," he acknowledges that the complexities and contexts of masculinity are bound up with that of the nation itself: "The question is this: How is an American to become a man? And this is precisely the same thing as asking: How is America to become a nation?" As examples he holds up "the tormented career of the author of Tom Sawyer" and "the beautiful ambiguity of the author of *Leaves of Grass*," Mark Twain and Walt Whitman respectively. Truth-teller that he was, Baldwin could not stop there but reaches back even further for the scene of the most masculine impulse—Genesis itself. "I beg you to remember …that troubling tree in Eden: it is 'the tree of the knowledge of good and evil.' What is meant by the masculine sensibility is the ability to eat the fruit of that tree, and live…indeed, one has no choice: eat, or die."

The withering impoverishment of masculine concepts and images can scarcely be abated; for a man's perceptions of himself, at least in America, often teeters on the "realities" of another. From "A Challenge to Bicentennial Candidates," he surmises that, for some men, the wages of blackness and "Americaness" are, in fact, madness. Consider this example:

> My father was a big, strong, handsome, healthy black man, who liked to use his muscles, who was accustomed to hard labor. He went mad and died in Bedlam because being black, he was always 'the last to be hired and the first to be fired.'

Again, Baldwin recalls and remembers, not for himself but for the benefit of others. "I am saddened indeed to be forced to recognize that my father's anguish—to say nothing of my brothers'—has cost the Republic so dearly." And this is the despair that has robbed America of untapped potential, intellect, and brilliance, all because the vessel is black. There is no way to count the numbers of dead black men that have been consumed by fear, treachery, and deception—each one a potential CEO, professor, or President.

Kenan readily admits that as he has lectured about Baldwin—his life and writings—one question resurrects itself again and again: "What would James Baldwin think of Barack Obama?" Most often, Kenan says, the question comes from "young people for whom the civil rights movement is a collection of pictures in a textbook." And why should they not ask such a question? Baldwin and Obama are linked by "a long arc of justice," one that summons the energies of an often dispossessed people. According to Baldwin, in "From Nationalism, Colonialism, and the United States: One Minute to Twelve—A Forum," " Robert Kennedy meagerly offered the opinion that, in 30 years' time, there could be a black president; Baldwin's response is neither conciliatory nor hopeful:

> …it has not entered the country's mind yet—that perhaps I wouldn't want to be [President]. And in any

case, what really exercises my mind is not this hypothetical day on which some other Negro "first" will become the first Negro President. What I am really curious about is just what kind of country he'll be President of.

Such questions about Obama are expected, but what excites me as a scholar of American culture—folk, pop, etc.—is what Baldwin would think of about the art, antics, and ascendancy of someone like Kanye West. Baldwin writes in "The Uses of the Blues" that "the acceptance of this anguish one finds in the blues, and the expression of it, creates also, however odd this may sound, a kind of joy." Could this sentiment explain the bipolarity of West, a man who is a walking metaphor of braggadocio, but who seems to exhibit time and again that his emotions are just below his skin? "Consider some of the things the blues are about," Baldwin writes. "They're about work, love, death, floods, lynchings; in fact, a series of disasters which can be summed up under the arbitrary heading 'Facts of Life.'" Listening to Kanye West's 808s and Heartbreak (2008), one cannot help understand it in the context of black folk music, which is to say that it is possibly one of the 21st century's thoroughly modern blues albums, situated squarely in the "gut-bucket" tradition of Bessie Smith, Leadbelly, and others, presenting an array of tracks that recall spirituals, work-songs, and gospels. West splays his heart for all to see; and the result is primitive, raw, and moving. Given the recent death of West's mother, his social awkwardness makes sense. West has a bad case of the blues. Perhaps this is why this particular essay provides an entrance into an overall critique of hip hop music and the culture it sells to its consumers, that crass materialism will provide happiness, that with a little "street savvy," one may, if one is lucky, re-invent one's very circumstances.

Kenan asks the reader step into Baldwin's shoes; it has a relatively redeeming appeal:

IMAGINE: It is 1947, late autumn. You are twenty-three years old. You are black…You wait tables. You have worked laying railroad tracks in New Jersey. You have hated the job. You hate segregated life and the indignities to which you were subjected on top of your hardscrabble existence. You cannot afford to go to college.

This type of empathetic strategy is brilliant, but it is a request that the reader is ultimately uncomfortable; for it asks the reader to consider the thrusts, concerns, and feelings a writer had toward himself but his subject, to feel how it felt to hate oneself and one's country. It is uneasy to vicariously predict the collapse the American empire. But "playing" Baldwin is not being Baldwin. The fact that Baldwin made it out of Harlem alive and sane is not only a miracle—it's an astronomical anomaly. Perhaps this is what troubles the reader—survivor's guilt—the same guilt that perturbed Baldwin as well.

The Voices of Boys To Men Project

The Journal of Black Masculinity, under the direction of Mrs. Pamela Fitzpatrick, doctoral student at the University of North Carolina at Greensboro and Literacy Coach at Orange County (North Carolina) Schools, is holding a writing contest for high school and college young men that offers them an exciting educational opportunity. We want to hear their fresh voices and their teachers celebrate their achievements as writers.

While we welcome any young man to submit writing pieces, we are especially interested in hearing from some male voices that have not historically been heard. We particularly want writing pieces from African American males, Latino males, Asian males, minority males, and poor/working class white males.

We are looking for a wide variety of male writing voices and a contemporary collection of genres, including the following types of writing pieces:

- **Short Stories**
- **Poetry**
- **Nonfiction**: Experiences of student life that other young people would find interesting
- **Rap Lyrics**: Songs that could be published in a journal for young adults
- **Book Reviews**: What are young men reading? What would interest other young men?
- **Movie Reviews**: What movies should other young people rush to see?

- **Art/Written Text Pieces**: Words, sentences, or paragraphs with artwork (Must be submitted digitally as a picture)

All entries must be received by *The Journal of Black Masculinity* by Tuesday, March 1. 2011. The contributions of contest winners will be featured in Vol. 1. No. 3 of *The Journal of Black Masculinity* and contributors will be invited to the University of North Carolina at Greensboro for a reception in the spring of 2011. For more information about submissions, please e-mail Mrs. Fitzpatrick at TVB2MNC@gmail.com.

Call for Papers -
The Philosophical Underpinnings of Gender Identity Journal of Black Masculinity Vol. 1, No. 4

Dr. Preston L. McKever-Floyd, Guest Editor

Know Thy Self is the perennial philosophical imperative that transcends time and cultures. The *self* to be found from antiquity to the modern era in Western culture, especially, was the *rational self.* This was the *self* that created the master narratives and was associated with the intellectually elite; all else were "other." Many feminist thinkers argue that the *rational self* maps white, elite, heterosexual male. The postmodern era fostered the deconstruction of master narratives and the elevation and validation of the previously marginalized narratives of the "other." Philosophically, the issue of personal identity, generally, and gendered identity, specifically, raises a number of questions: *If change is the primary characteristic of existence, does any "self" truly endure over time? Is the idea of gendered identity and illusion? Is gendered identity total identification with a body? Is there anything metaphysically "real" about gendered identity?* We invite papers from across disciplines that explore, but not limited to, to the following topics:

- ❖ Archetypes, stereotypes and gendered identity
- ❖ Hegemonic narratives and gendered identity
- ❖ Constructing and deconstructing gendered identity
- ❖ Gendered identity from the margins
- ❖ Gendered identity, permanent or fluid

Please submit manuscripts to <u>philoprof@yahoo.com</u>. The deadline for submissions is August 31, 2011.

Published by Peter Lang New York
Gause, C. P.
Integration Matters
Navigating Identity, Culture, and Resistance
New York, Bern, Berlin, Bruxelles, Frankfurt am Main,
Oxford, Wien, 2008. XVIII, 207 pp.

2009 Recipient of the American Educational Studies
Association (AESA) Critics Choice Award

Counterpoints, Studies in the Postmodern Theory of Education
Vol. 337
Edited by Joe Kincheloe / Shirley Steinberg

ISBN 978-1-4331-0202-8pb.
Order online: www.peterlang.com
SFR 33.00 / €* 22.70 / €** 23.30 / € 21.20 / £ 15.90 / US-$ 32.95

The United States is more racially, culturally, and linguistically diverse now than at any given point in its history. Urbanization and immigration are key contributors to population growth and shifts, particularly in the southeastern part of the country. Educators are scrambling to determine how best to serve different demographics and many families in new places are trying to adjust to unfamiliar school systems. For all concerned, this period of adjustment is marked by significant personal, curricular, and institutional development. However, one group of individuals has not maintained pace with the rest: African American males continue to lag behind their counterparts in every measured educational variable as outlined by the No Child Left Behind legislation, despite the educational, social, and economic changes of the past fifty years (since the 1954 landmark Brown vs. Board of Education decision).
This book - beyond providing educators, parents, and students with a critique of present day educational experiences for those who are the

«other» in America, particularly the black male - conceptually integrates queer legal theory, the tenets of critical spirituality, and notions of collaborative activism to construct a blueprint for realizing academic achievement and academic success for all students.

Carlson, Dennis / Gause, C. P. (eds.)
Keeping the Promise
Essays on Leadership, Democracy, and Education
New York, Bern, Berlin, Bruxelles, Frankfurt am Main, Oxford, Wien, 2007. XVIII, 416 pp.

2007 Recipient of the American Educational Studies Association (AESA) Critics Choice Award

Counterpoints, Studies in the Postmodern Theory of Education
Vol. 305
Edited by Shirley Steinberg

ISBN 978-0-8204-8199-9 pub.
Order online: www.peterlang.com
SFR 37.00 / €* 25.50 / €** 26.20 / € 23.80 / £ 21.40 / US-$ 36.95
This volume raises critical questions about the qualities of democratic educational leadership during a time when the promise of democratic education and public life risks being abandoned, forgotten, and emptied of meaning. A diverse chorus of scholars in education takes on this issue by analyzing the cultural context of educational leadership in the age of No Child Left Behind, by offering democratic counter-narratives of educational leadership, and by deconstructing popular culture representations of educational leaders. In doing so, they re-situate leadership within a political context and link it to struggles over social justice and human freedom.

The contributing scholars also radically re-think educational leadership in ways that include teachers, university-based educators, and scholars as leaders.

Contents:

Dennis Carlson/Charles P. Gause: Introduction

Dennis Carlson: Are We Making Progress? The Discursive Construction of Progress in the Age of «No Child Left Behind»

Michael W. Apple: Schooling, Markets, Race, and an Audit Culture

Richard A. Quantz: Leadership, Culture, and Democracy: Rethinking Systems and Conflict in Schools

Jackie M. Blount: Some Historical Tensions about Sexuality and Gender in Schools

Valerie Scatamburlo-D'Annibale/Juha Suoranta/Peter McLaren: Excavating Hope among the Ruins: Confronting Creeping Fascism in Our Midst

Catherine A. Lugg: Sissies, Faggots, Lezzies, and Dykes: Gender, Sexual Orientation, and a New Politics of Education? –

Michael E. Dantley: Re-Radicalizing the Consciousness in Educational Leadership: The Critically Spiritual Imperative toward Keeping the Promise

Joanne Chesley: Student Engagement and Academic Achievement: A Promising Connection

Camille Wilson Cooper/Charles P. Gause: «Who's Afraid of the Big Bad Wolf?» Facing Identity Politics and Resistance When Teaching for Social Justice

Charles P. Gause/Ulrich C. Reitzug/Leila E. Villaverde: Beyond Generic Democracy: Holding Our Students Accountable for Democratic Leadership and Practice

Kathleen Knight Abowitz/Kate Rousmaniere: Margaret Haley as Diva: A Case Study of a Feminist Citizen-Leader

Rochelle Garner: Unpacking on a Long Journey Home: A Lesson on Race, Identity, and Culture

Lauri Johnson: Making Her Community a Better Place to Live: Lessons from History for Culturally Responsive Urban School Leadership

Lori Chajet: The Power and Limits of Small School Reform: Institutional Agency and Democratic Leadership in Public Education

Michelle Fine: Resisting the Passive Revolution: Democratic, Participatory Research by Youth

Stephanie A. Flores-Koulish: Media Literacy: An Entrée for Pre-service Teachers into Critical Pedagogy?

Glenn M. Hudak: Leadership-With: A Spiritual Perspective on Professional & Revolutionary Leadership in a Digital Culture

Linda C. Tillman: Halls of Anger: The (Mis)Representation of African American Principals in Film

James Trier: Critically Examining Popular Culture Representations of Educators.

JBM Style Guide: Making it Look Good

Jean K. Rosales, Ph.D.
University of North Carolina, Greensboro

Abstract

This is where your abstract should go. Note there is a 12 pt. space after the Abstract title. Do not indent the first line. Note also that if your abstract contains a book title, such as The Wizard of Oz, *or a movie title, such as* The Silence of the Lambs, *that would be italicized in normal text, it should be formatted as normal text (no italics) in the abstract.*

Introduction

The first line of this paragraph and all paragraphs in normal text should be indented 0.5 and entered in Times New Roman 12 pt., justified, with single spacing. Please do not enter spaces between paragraphs. Periods and colons should be followed by two spaces.

Level 1 Headings

The first level heading is in Times New Roman, 12 pt., bold, centered. There is a 12-point space before and a 12-point space after.

About Level 2 Headings

Level 2 headings are in Times New Roman, 12 pt., italic, flush left. There is a 12-point space before and a 12-point space after.

Quotations

Short quotations

If you are quoting an excerpt of fewer than 3 lines (approximately 40 words), the text should remain in the body of the paragraph, set off with double quote marks. According to Rosales (2010), "The best way to use quotes is sparingly but accurately" (p. 5). Note that the page citation appears in parentheses and that the final period for the sentence *follows* the page citation. If your signal sentence does not include a citation for the author, you can add it at the end of the sentence like this (Rosales, 2010, p. 5). The page number for the inline citation does not have to include a page number if you are not quoting the author directly.

Longer quotations (block quotes)

If you are excerpting 3 or more lines, you should use a block quote format. This is indented 0.5 on the left and 0.5 on the right. It should not begin with quotation marks unless the excerpt you are using has quotation marks in it. Thus, according to Rosales (2010):

> The excerpt is indented and should reproduce the original text as closely as possible. If you decide to *emphasize* the material by adding italics, note this by including the phrase "emphasis added" as soon as practical without interrupting the flow of your quotation (emphasis added). If all of the emphasis was added by

you, it is acceptable to note this with the page citation at the end of the paragraph. (p. 8, emphasis added)

Note that a block quote as above is preceded by a 12-point space and followed by a 12-point space. Note also that ALL block quotes must have a page citation. If the source citation identifying the author(s) and year is not included in the phrase leading up to the block quotes, it should be inserted at the end of the block quote as above.

Referring to other works

If you are citing the title of a longer source, such as a book, movie, or television series, capitalize all words of four or more letters and use italics, so a reference to *The Ultimate Guide to Submitting an Article* would look like this. Note again that, in the Abstract section of your article, since the base font is italic, references to longer sources should appear in plain (no italicized) text.

If you are citing a shorter source, such as a journal article, song title, episode of a television series, or short poem, capitalize all words of four or more letters and enclose the title in double quotes, so a reference to "Guidelines for JBM Authors" would look like this.

Unusual Spellings, Capitalization or Punctuation

We generally follow the guidelines of the *APA Publication Manual*. However, we are also sensitive to authors' desire to use unusual spelling, capitalization and/or punctuation in their works, particularly in emerging fields of study such as black masculinity, women's studies, and queer studies. You can signal your intention to use unusual formatting by inserting a comment in a Word file move your cursor over the yellow area to view the comment) or by inserting the word [stet] in square brackets after your first use of the unique item. (The "stet" will be removed by our copyeditor prior to publication.)

As a courtesy to our copyeditor, if you are quoting an author who uses unusual spelling, capitalization or punctuation in the material you are quoting, please also insert a comment as above to verify the intentional deviation from APA style.

Please also note that our copyeditor does not routinely receive copies of communication between you and other editors or reviewers, so she will not know about any comments you may have made to them about intentional deviations in those communications.

Deviations will be corrected to follow APA Style if comments are not included with the text of your submission.

Graphic Material

You are welcome to include graphics in your submission. You should be aware, however, that *JBM* is printed and distributed in black and white. Therefore, all graphs, charts, and other illustrative materials will be reproduced in grayscale. It is helpful, therefore, to use patterns rather than colors to distinguish between areas of the graph like sections of a pie chart or bars on a bar graph. Please also include a caption in your graphic such as Figure 1: My Extremely Interesting Data. The caption should appear in 12 point Times New Roman and be centered beneath the graph. If possible, to maintain a consistent look, labels on your graph should be entered in 12 point Times New Roman font.

All graphic material should fit into a space not exceeding 5.0 inches in width and 6.0 inches in height. If your graphic exceeds these limits, the figure will be resized or rotated to fit the space available.

Poems and Other Artistic Materials

The Journal of Black Masculinity welcomes submissions of poetry or other artistic material. Please submit your material in 12 point Times New Roman font and indent it 0.5 inches on the left and right (as if it were a block quote). You may use textboxes in Microsoft Word to achieve exact placement of text blocks as needed. If you have special layout needs, please advise the editor of this requirement and provide detailed instructions for laying out your material. *JBM* does not have specialized typesetting equipment and we cannot honor requests to insert special symbols in your text. You can contact *JBM*'s editor, Dr. C. P. Gause, at drcpgause@gmail.com to discuss special concerns and subscription rates. The copyeditor is not authorized to provide specialized typesetting services for submissions. The *Journal of Black Masculinity* is not responsible for the views expressed by individuals in articles published in this journal.

JBM Style Guide—Technical Summary

Margins
Left margin: 1.5
Right margin: 1.5
Bottom: 1.5
Top: 1.0
Header: 0.5" from top
Footer: 0.7" from bottom

Headers
You may omit headers; they will be added by the copyeditor
All headers are 0.5" from top
First page header: Journal of Black Masculinity, Vol. 1, No. 1, 16 pt., italic, Times New Roman, centered
Odd page header: Short title of article, 12 pt., Times New Roman, italic, centered

Even page header: Journal of Black Masculinity, Vol. 1, No. 1, 12 pt., italic, Times New Roman, centered

Footers
You may omit footers; they will be added by the copyeditor
All footers are 0.7" from bottom, 12 pt., Times New Roman, centered

Text Styles
All fonts are Times New Roman

Abstract: Use Heading 1 for "Abstract," text is Times New Roman, 12 pt., italic, justified, single space, don't add space between paragraphs of the same style

Author and affiliation: Times New Roman, 14 pt., left aligned, single space, don't add space between paragraphs of the same style

Bibliography entries: Times New Roman, 12 pt. bold, justified, single space, hanging indent at 0.5, no space before or after; follow APA Publication Manual, 5th or 6th editions (see below for examples)

Bibliography title: Times New Roman, 12 pt. bold, centered, single space, 24 pt. space before, 12 pt. space after

Block Quote: Times New Roman, 12 pt., justified, indent 0.5 left and right (mirror indents), single space, 12 pt. space before, 12 pt. space after

Heading 1: Times New Roman, 12 pt. bold, centered, single space, 12 pt. space before, 12 pt. space after
Heading 2: Times New Roman, 12 pt. bold italic, left aligned, single space, 12 pt. space before, 12 pt. space after

Normal (body text): Times New Roman, 12 pt., justified, single space, don't add space between paragraphs of the same style; begin new paragraphs with 0.5" indent

Notes: Do not use footnotes; endnotes may be used if necessary, number beginning with 1, followed by a period and 2 spaces, Times New Roman, 12 pt., justified, hanging indent 0.5, single space. Use Heading 2 formatting for section heading "Notes."

Quote (block quote): Times New Roman, 12 pt., justified, indent 0.5 left and right (mirror indents), single space, 12 pt. space before, 12 pt. space after. Punctuation for the final sentence is inserted before the author/page citation.

Title: Times New Roman, 18 pt., bold, centered, single space, 30 pt. space before, 18 pt. space after

Graphics

JBM is published in black and white; therefore, figures such as charts submitted in color will be reproduced in grayscale. For clearer definition, it is recommended that the graphic designer use patterns, rather than color, to distinguish between sections of the chart or graph.

Graphics should not exceed 5 inches in width and 6 inches in height. If a graphic cannot fit into this specification, it may have to be reduced or rotated on the page.

Recommended Formatting for Bibliographic Entries (APA Publication Manual)

All references should use a hanging indent of 0.5 inches. If you cannot use hanging indent formatting, enter straight text. Do not use carriage returns and tabs to simulate a hanging indent; it is more time-consuming to remove them than it is to reformat the paragraph. Text should be justified *except* when citing a URL. Insert a carriage return prior to the URL as needed to avoid excessive spacing in the main citation and insert a tab of 0.5 to indent this line. Use single-space line spacing for bibliographic entries. Do not enter a space between entries.

General style for formatting with respect to capitalization, italicization, and punctuation follows APA guidelines. **Note that *JBM* does not follow APA style guidelines in the matter of authors' first names.** The APA recommends using initials only; we find that this practice makes it more difficult for readers to follow up on and locate cited works. Therefore, you are encouraged to include the entire name of authors, including first names when commonly used, in bibliographic entries when possible.

Bibliography

Aardvark, Ann. (1997). Best places to find edible insects. *Aardvark Quarterly 72* (3), 12-15.

Lennon, John, & McCartney, Paul. (1967). "I Am The Walrus." *Magical Mystery Tour.* Capitol Records.

Gause, C. P. (2010). *The Professor's Closet.* Greensboro: Way To Go Publications.

Rosales, Jean. (2007). Lockkeeper's House.
Retrieved from: http://www.kittytours.org

Rosales, Jean, & Jobe, Michael. (2003). Fun Stuff. *DC Goes to the Movies.* Pocatello, ID: iPublish.

Simon, David (Producer), & Wilson, Clark (Director). (2003). The End [Television series episode]. In David Smith, (Producer), *The Wire.* Los Angeles: HBO Series.

Smith, Snuffy (Producer), & Wesson, Oyle (Director). (2008). *Big Gay Movie* [Motion picture]. United States: Pictures of Color.

A useful resource for APA citation style is available at
http://owl.english.purdue.edu/owl.

Citations in your text and bibliography will be reviewed and edited as needed by the *JBM* copyeditor. If you are unsure of how to format a bibliographic item, provide as much information as you can on the work being cited and our copyeditor will reformat for you.

Affiliation and Biography

Please include an affiliation note that will appear with your name at the beginning of your submission. This can be an institution such as a college, university, nonprofit organization, or other entity with which you want to be identified. If you prefer to not provide this sort of entity, please include the city and state (or country) in which you normally reside.

At the end of your submission, we will include a biography of approximately 50 words. You may include contact information, such as an address, e-mail address, and/or phone number. Keep in mind this information will be published and be aware of the possibility that identity theft and spam can be results of your sharing Too Much Information.

LaVergne, TN USA
02 February 2011
214944LV00004B/45/P